W9-CEI-371

Ex-Library: Friends of
Lake County Public Library

The Titanic

Titles in the World History Series

The Titanic

by Victoria Sherrow

Lucent Books, P.O. Box 289011, San Diego, CA 92198-9011

LAKE COUNTY PUBLIC LIBRARY

3 3113 01816 4287

Library of Congress Cataloging-in-Publication Data

Sherrow, Victoria.
    The Titanic / Victoria Sherrow.
        p. cm.—(World history series)
    Includes bibliographical references and index.
    Summary: Describes the planning and building of the
Titanic, its departure and passengers, its fatal collision with
an iceberg and sinking, and the fascination with this disaster
held by so many people.
    ISBN 1-56006-472-2   (lib. : alk. paper)
    1. Titanic (Steamship)—Juvenile literature.
2. Shipwrecks—North Atlantic Ocean—Juvenile literature.
[1. Titanic (Steamship) 2. Shipwrecks.]   I. Title. II. Series.
G530.T6S48   1999
910'.9163'4—dc21   98–43466
                                                         CIP
                                                          AC

Copyright 1999 by Lucent Books, Inc., P.O. Box 289011,
San Diego, California 92198-9011

Printed in the U.S.A.

No part of this book may be reproduced or used in any other
form or by any other means, electrical, mechanical, or otherwise, including, but not limited to, photocopy, recording, or
any information storage and retrieval system, without prior written permission from the publisher.

Contents

Foreword

Each year on the first day of school, nearly every history teacher faces the task of explaining why his or her students should study history. One logical answer to this question is that exploring what happened in our past explains how the things we often take for granted—our customs, ideas, and institutions—came to be. As statesman and historian Winston Churchill put it, "Every nation or group of nations has its own tale to tell. Knowledge of the trials and struggles is necessary to all who would comprehend the problems, perils, challenges, and opportunities which confront us today." Thus, a study of history puts modern ideas and institutions in perspective. For example, though the founders of the United States were talented and creative thinkers, they clearly did not invent the concept of democracy. Instead, they adapted some democratic ideas that had originated in ancient Greece and with which the Romans, the British, and others had experimented. An exploration of these cultures, then, reveals their very real connection to us through institutions that continue to shape our daily lives.

Another reason often given for studying history is the idea that lessons exist in the past from which contemporary societies can benefit and learn. This idea, although controversial, has always been an intriguing one for historians. Those who agree that society can benefit from the past often quote philosopher George Santayana's famous statement, "Those who cannot remember the past are condemned to repeat it." Historians who subscribe to Santayana's philosophy believe that, for example, studying the events that led up to the major world wars or other significant historical events would allow society to chart a different and more favorable course in the future.

Just as difficult as convincing students to realize the importance of studying history is the search for useful and interesting supplementary materials that present historical events in a context that can be easily understood. The volumes in Lucent Books' World History Series attempt to present a broad, balanced, and penetrating view of the march of history. Ancient Egypt's important wars and rulers, for example, are presented against the rich and colorful backdrop of Egyptian religious, social, and cultural developments. The series engages the reader by enhancing historical events with these cultural contexts. For example, in *Ancient Greece*, the text covers the role of women in that society. Slavery is discussed in *The Roman Empire*, as well as how slaves earned their freedom. The numerous and varied aspects of everyday life in these and other societies are explored in each volume of the series. Additionally, the series covers the major political, cultural, and philosophical ideas as the torch of civilization is passed from ancient Mesopotamia and Egypt, through Greece, Rome, Medieval Europe, and other world cultures, to the modern day.

The material in the series is formatted in a thorough, precise, and organized manner. Each volume offers the reader a comprehensive and clearly written overview of an important historical event or period. The topic under discussion is placed in a broad historical context. For example, *The Italian Renaissance* begins with a discussion of the High Middle Ages and the loss of central control that allowed certain Italian cities to develop artistically. The book ends by looking forward to the Reformation and interpreting the societal changes that grew out of the Renaissance. Thus, students are not only involved in an historical era, but also enveloped by the events leading up to that era and the events following it.

One important and unique feature in the World History Series is the primary and secondary source quotations that richly supplement each volume. These quotes are useful in a number of ways. First, they allow students access to sources they would not normally be exposed to because of the difficulty and obscurity of the original source. The quotations range from interesting anecdotes to farsighted cultural perspectives and are drawn from historical witnesses both past and present. Second, the quotes demonstrate how and where historians themselves derive their information on the past as they strive to reach a consensus on historical events. Lastly, all of the quotes are footnoted, familiarizing students with the citation process and allowing them to verify quotes and/or look up the original source if the quote piques their interest.

Finally, the books in the World History Series provide a detailed launching point for further research. Each book contains a bibliography specifically geared toward student research. A second, annotated bibliography introduces students to all the sources the author consulted when compiling the book. A chronology of important dates gives students an overview, at a glance, of the topic covered. Where applicable, a glossary of terms is included.

In short, the series is designed not only to acquaint readers with the basics of history, but also to make them aware that their lives are a part of an ongoing human saga. Perhaps they will then come to the same realization as famed historian Arnold Toynbee. In his monumental work, *A Study of History,* he wrote about becoming aware of history flowing through him in a mighty current, and of his own life "welling like a wave in the flow of this vast tide."

Important Dates in the History of the Titanic

1870   1899   1906   1907   1908   1909   1911   1912   1935   1985   1986   1997

1870
The White Star Line joins forces with the shipbuilding firm Harland & Wolff.

1899
Thomas Ismay, chairman of the White Star Line, dies; his son, J. Bruce, becomes the new chairman.

1906
International Mercantile Marine (IMM) buys the White Star Line; William James Pirrie becomes chairman of Harland & Wolff.

1907
The Cunard Line, White Star's main competitor, produces the *Lusitania* and *Mauretania*, faster than any White Star liners.

1908
J. Bruce Ismay approves designs for three new, giant liners to be named *Olympic*, *Titanic*, and *Gigantic*.

1909
The keels of the sister ships *Olympic* and *Titanic* are completed.

May 31, 1911
The *Titanic* is launched; the *Olympic* sets out on its maiden voyage.

April 10, 1912
The *Titanic* departs on its maiden voyage from the port at Southampton, England; later that day, it stops in Cherbourg, France.

April 12, 1912
The *Titanic* receives the first of nine warnings regarding ice in that region of the North Atlantic.

April 14, 1912
Near midnight, the *Titanic* strikes an iceberg causing fatal damage to the hull.

April 15, 1912
The *Titanic* sinks at about 2:10 A.M.; At 4:10 A.M., the *Carpathia* reaches the first lifeboat and begins taking on survivors.

1935
The *Olympic* is retired from service; the White Star Line soon merges with Cunard to become the White Star-Cunard Lines.

1985
A joint American-French oceanographic expedition locates the remains of the *Titanic*.

1986
U.S. oceanographers aboard the submersible *Alvin* explore the *Titanic*.

1997
The film *Titanic* becomes the largest grossing movie in history and brings renewed interest in the tragedy.

"Ship of Dreams"

On July 20, 1986, three oceanographers operating an underwater submarine named *Alvin* finished another day's work at the bottom of the North Atlantic. For a week they had been exploring and photographing the site of a massive, tragic shipwreck.

Amid the ship's rusted remains they found thousands of different objects: lumps of coal for fuel, wine bottles, china and silverware, cooking pots, bathtubs, chairs, light fixtures, suitcases, doorknobs, part of a child's porcelain doll, men's boots. These and many more such items lay strewn on the ocean floor, where they had sunk with the *Titanic.* They were grim reminders that more than one thousand men, women, and children had died there.

Before they left the ocean floor that day, the scientists placed a memorial plaque on the once-great ship's ravaged stern. The plaque, donated by the Titanic Historical Society, commemorated "those souls who perished with the *Titanic,* April 14–15, 1912." As Robert D. Ballard, the scientist who led the oceanographic expedition, later wrote,

> Those who had died had gathered on the stern as the ship had tilted bow first. This had been their final haven. So we rose up the wall of steel to the top of the stern. With great care, *Alvin's*

mechanical arm plucked the plaque from where it had been strapped . . . and gently released it. We watched as it sank quietly to the deck of the stern.[1]

The *Titanic* was named for the Titans, mighty gods of Greek mythology renowned for their size and strength. The name had seemed fitting when the White Star Line had set out in 1907 to create a towering ship that would impress the world's most demanding travelers. Their new luxury liner was advertised as "the Ship of Dreams," "the Ship of Wonders," and "the Floating Palace." After April 15, 1912, however, the word *Titanic* would come to signify disaster.

When she left port that April, the R.M.S. (Royal Mail ship) *Titanic* was the largest moving object ever built. The ship's engines were four stories high. Each propeller was as tall as a house. The sixteen compartments inside the hull had each been designed to be watertight, with doors that would close at the touch of a switch. Journalists called the *Titanic* a triumph of modern engineering. A respected British technical journal, *Shipbuilder,* argued that the ship had been made "practically unsinkable."[2]

An excited public had followed the progress of the enormous ship as thousands of workers built it over a three-year period. Thousands more came to see it launched from its Irish shipyard in 1911. People around the world watched newsreels about the *Titanic* and pored over photographs that showed her lavish First Class staterooms, grand staircase, glass-domed promenade, and swimming pool. From humble beginnings, travel on the high seas had now reached astonishing heights.

The first steamship lines began carrying passengers across the Atlantic during the 1840s. These voyages were marked by tossing ships, watery decks, and cramped cabins. Worst of all were the steerage spaces, located at the bottom of the ship, which were dark, damp, and noisy.

Steamships made their profits both from carrying mail from one continent to the other and by taking up passenger fares. As the industry grew, new companies sprang up to transport increasing numbers of passengers. Along with immigrants resettling in the New World, more people were now crossing the Atlantic regularly for business or pleasure. Wealthy Americans enjoyed touring Europe, with its many cultural attractions, as well as visiting more exotic countries like Egypt. These upper-class Americans had inherited fortunes or amassed them in industry, mining, real estate, and investments, for example.

During what the author Mark Twain called the Gilded Age, the 1890s, wealthy people lived and traveled in a style that is rarely, if ever, seen today. They could afford to, and did, travel often, taking along servants and masses of luggage. Wealthy Europeans, often of noble birth, joined these Americans at fashionable hotels in Paris and London and at fabulous resorts and spas in Germany, Switzerland, and the

The Titanic's *grand staircase offers a glimpse of the opulence that the luxury liner's First Class passengers traveled in.*

Dreaming of New Lives

Fear and hope pervaded the steerage sections of ships traveling from Europe to America at the turn of the century. But there was often gaiety, as well, as passengers sang and danced to the familiar music of bagpipes, fiddles, and other instruments.

Various laws required the steamship companies to screen people before taking them to America. The companies checked potential passengers for contagious diseases and tried to determine if they were criminals. It was worthwhile to do so, because if the passengers did not pass inspection upon their arrival in the United States, the shipping lines were required to take them back at company expense. The U.S. government also fined the lines $100 for each immigrant found unqualified to enter the United States.

As a result, the shipping lines implemented policies to keep their passengers healthy. One passenger from Ireland to New York recalled being forced to have a health inspection and take a shower before boarding the ship. Ticket holders were deloused in a special hotel run by the shipping company, both when they arrived at the docks and when they went to board their ship. Their baggage was also fumigated. When they arrived in America they had to shower again and were subjected to careful medical examinations.

The quarters in steerage were tight, and passengers often slept in their clothing. Storms could be terrifying. A woman who emigrated from Sweden at the age of six later recalled a serious storm at sea: "There was a lot of crying and people were saying, 'We're never going to reach America.'"

The famous British author Robert Louis Stevenson, who habitually traveled Second Class, made a point of visiting the steerage section on the ship. As he once wrote: "The stench was atrocious. To descend on an empty stomach was an adventure." In 1908 an inspector from the U.S. Immigration Commission traveled undercover in steerage to expose conditions there. As he reported: "It is a congestion so intense, so injurious to the health and morals that there is nothing on land to equal it. . . . Everything was dirty, sticky, and disagreeable to the touch."

When they finally entered New York harbor and saw the Statue of Liberty, people often wept, shouted with joy, or sang songs of thanksgiving. Some waved their arms in the direction of the statue, convinced that freedom and opportunity must surely lie around the corner.

White Star, the shipping company that owned the Titanic, *furnished the ship so lavishly that it was referred to as a floating palace.*

south of France. In the United States, millionaires often spent the summer in Newport, Rhode Island, or other fashionable seaside towns.

Airline travel did not exist then, so all transatlantic trips were necessarily by sea. Author Michael Davie has noted that "the liners carried Americans to Europe in search of pleasure, culture, health cures, and titled husbands and Britons to the United States in search of business, relatives who had emigrated and prospered, and fees from lecture tours."[3]

Affluent travelers wanted fast ships with the elegant accommodations and excellent service they were accustomed to receiving at the best hotels. Shipping companies obliged by competing for their business,

offering spacious First Class suites and staterooms on the upper decks. Dining salons and other public rooms were enlarged and beautifully appointed. There travelers could meet with friends to enjoy fine meals and entertainment while showing off their elegant clothes and jewels. They did not have to mingle with people of a lower socioeconomic status.

Less affluent people continued to cross the ocean too. The industrial revolution had increased the demand for workers in America. During the late 1800s and early 1900s, cheap labor was needed in America's mills, mines, stockyards, and factories. Tens of thousands of workers were required to help construct railroads, bridges, and buildings in growing cities. The majority of these workers came from Europe. By the turn of the century, most of these immigrants were coming from southern and eastern Europe, as well as from northern and western European countries.

Poorer travelers booked Third Class rooms in the bottom and rear of the ship, called steerage, because this area had once been used to carry cattle. The steerage compartment was noisy, crowded, and rarely clean. Immigrants who hoped for a new and better life in America were nevertheless willing to endure these hardships.

Keen Competition

As the century progressed, the number of people seeking to cross the Atlantic continued to grow. During the 1870s, more than 400,000 people arrived in New York harbor each year. The steamship lines competed for both the wealthy and the immigrant trade. Passengers could choose from eleven major shipping lines.

As shipping companies tried to lure more and more passengers, profits became a major focus. Passengers' desires and expectations influenced the shipbuilding industry. To attract the wealthy, designers added elegant staircases and grand reception rooms, and enlarged the passengers' staterooms. In order to provide space for these amenities and better contact between passengers and the crew who served them on board, builders sacrificed certain safety features, such as watertight decks and double hulls.

The two top shipping lines, Cunard and White Star, each sought to operate the most desirable ships. The White Star Line took the lead in 1912 when it introduced its *Titanic*, a "Floating Palace" fit for the kings of finance and industry and the titled people of the world.

Rich and poor alike, however, would sail on the ship's one and only voyage, in April 1912. A fatal combination of shortcomings in design, human error, and forces of nature would converge to sink the mighty ship, culminating in a tragedy that continues to haunt people today. With the loss of the *Titanic*, an old and more stable era seemed to come to an end, ushering in more uncertain times.

1 Twenty-Five Thousand Tons of Steel

A team of twenty horses tramped along the streets of Belfast, Ireland, lugging a wagon with an enormous object chained across its flat top. The object weighed fifteen and a half tons, about thirty-one thousand pounds. It was an anchor, the largest of three that would be used on the *Titanic*, then under construction at the local Harland & Wolff Shipyards. Together the three anchors would weigh more than thirty tons.

To curious onlookers the anchor looked immense, but then everything about the new ship seemed larger than life. The *Titanic* would eventually cost £1.5 million (about $7 million). Three thousand skilled laborers worked nearly three years to complete the ship, which required twenty-five thousand tons of steel and huge amounts of other materials and supplies, including plumbing fixtures, generators, wood, tiles, caulking, cables, cement, and paint. It would be the largest, grandest ship White Star shipping lines had ever commissioned.

Larger, Faster, Better

The idea for this giant ship came from Lord Pirrie, chairman of Harland & Wolff, and J. (Joseph) Bruce Ismay, manager of the White Star Line. At age fifteen, William

James Pirrie had begun his career as a draftsman apprentice at Harland & Wolff after he and his widowed mother left his native Canada for Ireland, where his Scottish ancestors had lived. Pirrie became head designer at his Belfast firm and, by 1874, a partner at the age of twenty-seven. After he rose to the position of chairman in 1906, Pirrie embarked on a two-year modernization program.

J. Bruce Ismay's father, Thomas Ismay, had founded the White Star Line during the mid-1800s. In 1870, White Star began working with Harland & Wolff. Together they produced the *Oceanic*. In 1889, White Star launched the first modern ocean liners without sails—the *Teutonic* and *Majestic*—both built by Harland & Wolff.

After Thomas Ismay died in 1899, the company fulfilled his plans to build four large passenger liners that would stress comfort, White Star's trademark, more than speed. White Star also took pride in its safety record. Between 1902 and 1912, the company carried 2,179,594 passengers. Only two people had died at sea, both when the *Republic* collided with the *Florida* in 1902.

The four new ships—the *Cedric*, *Celtic*, *Baltic*, and *Adriatic*—were completed between 1901 and 1907, bringing White Star a larger following and more prestige.

White Star's main competitor, the Cunard Line, produced the *Lusitania* and *Mauretania* in 1907. These two beautiful ships, which featured steam turbine engines, were the fastest, largest ships in operation. They captivated wealthy and influential people on both sides of the Atlantic.

White Star responded by building the *Megantic* and *Laurentic*. By this time, competition was even more intense, because German luxury liners had begun operating in the North Atlantic during the 1890s.

A major reason for creating larger ships was to accommodate more emigrants. In 1907 alone, more than 1 million people came to the United States, and transporting them was a lucrative business. In addition, about 100,000 people left America each year to return home to Europe. Because the shipping lines could not predict the number of immigrants or returnees who would book passage, they sought to attract as many other kinds of passengers as possible. Ship designers had to consider all these factors if they hoped to stay in business.

In 1907, Pirrie (who had been knighted in 1906 and was now Lord Pirrie) and J. Bruce Ismay decided to build three gigantic new White Star ships that would outclass the other transatlantic liners. They met at Pirrie's home one evening to discuss these plans after dinner. The new ships would be called the *Olympic*, *Titanic*, and *Gigantic* (later renamed the *Britannic*). No expense was to be spared, no corners cut, in their construction.

By the time White Star envisioned these steam liners, the company had more money at its disposal. The American financier John Pierpont (J. P.) Morgan and other wealthy investors had founded International Mercantile Marine (IMM), a huge

American financier John Pierpont (J. P.) Morgan and fellow investors purchased the White Star Line in 1906 for $25 million in gold.

shipping company, at the turn of the century. Morgan, trying to monopolize the transatlantic passenger trade, had almost put Cunard out of business by lowering the price of steerage tickets to only £2. The British government rescued Cunard with financial aid, which the company used to good advantage.

In 1906, IMM bought the White Star Line for $25 million in gold. Although most people continued to regard White Star as a British company, the American trust now owned it. J. P. Morgan's group of investors approved plans for the three new ships.

Building a Giant

To prepare for the construction of these ships, Harland & Wolff acquired new equipment and expanded their facilities. A special extra-strength slip was constructed, along with a 220-foot-high gantry crane. Larger spaces were created to make the oversized ships' boilers.

Dozens of designers worked in the brightly lit drafting room at the shipyard to create mechanical plans for the first ship, the *Olympic*, and her sister ship, the *Titanic*. Thomas Andrews, Lord Pirrie's nephew, headed the design department. Known for his sense of humor and fair mindedness, Andrews was liked and respected by management and workers alike. He often arrived as early as 4:00 A.M., wearing his signature paint-spattered hat. One foreman who worked at the plant called Andrews "one of nature's gentlemen."[4] The White Star crews also loved Andrews, who treated them with courtesy and consideration.

Lord Pirrie's brother-in-law Alexander Carlisle also worked at Harland & Wolff. Carlisle oversaw the interior design and decoration for the new ships.

In July 1908, Ismay inspected and approved the designs for his company's new liners. The next year, the keels of the first two ships were laid. The public was awed when the splendid *Olympic* was launched on October 20, 1910.

Work continued on the *Titanic*, destined to outshine even the *Olympic*. As with earlier White Star liners, the ship was designed and constructed with great care. For safety reasons, the *Titanic*'s hull was made with two coats of steel, called a double bottom. It rose seven feet above the keel and had an outer skin one inch thick. The hull contained sixteen compartments, which the designers declared watertight.

These compartments were divided by fifteen crosswise bulkheads that extended far above the waterline. The captain could close the compartment doors by moving an electrical switch located on the bridge.

When it was launched in April 1912, the Titanic *was the largest moving object ever built. It took 25,000 tons of steel, three thousand workers, and three years to complete.*

Three Million Rivets

Like other parts of the *Titanic*, its rivets, iron bolts with a head on one end that were used to hold the ship's steel plates together, were large—a full three inches long. Dick Sweeney, an employee at Harland & Wolff whose father and grandfather worked on the *Titanic*, told Michael Davie, author of *Titanic: The Death and Life of a Legend*, about the painstaking work required to rivet the ship by hand:

> They started at six in the morning and went on until half past five at night, working in squads of four. First the heater boys heated up the rivets. They were called heater boys but they might be fifty. They had a long pair of tongs and they poked the rivets into a coke brazier for three or four minutes, keeping the brazier hot by working a bellows with their foot. Then they threw the rivet to a "catch boy" and he put the stalk of the rivet into a hole through two overlapping plates. Then a man called the "holder up" put a big heavy hammer under the panhead on the rivet, which was of pure iron, and held on to it while the fourth man beat it and flattened it into the hole. The outside hull, the shell, was worked on by special men called "shell-riveters," and the men who hammered in the rivets were divided into the right-handers and the left-handers. . . . They used a sledge hammer weighing about five pounds. . . . They'd do about 200 rivets a day . . . provided it didn't rain.
>
> At day's end an inspector moved along the inside of the hull with a hammer, tapping to make sure the rivets were securely in place.

The designers believed that even if two compartments were completely filled with water, the ship would not sink. Nobody envisioned an accident that would cause even this much damage.

Plans were made to float the hull of the *Titanic* on May 31, 1911, ready for completion. The *Olympic* was scheduled to be ready for its first voyage on the very same day.

A Festive Launching

The White Star Line did not welcome its new ships with a traditional christening ceremony of breaking a bottle of champagne against the bow. Nonetheless, the *Olympic* and, later, the *Titanic* were launched with great fanfare. On the morning of

The Titanic

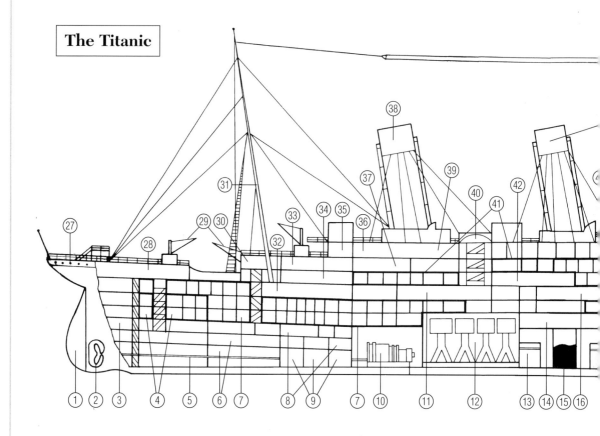

1. Rudder
2. Propeller (one of three)
3. Cargo Holds
4. Third Class Berths/Steerage
5. Propeller Shaft Tunnel
6. Refrigerated Cargo
7. State Rooms, Second Class
8. Ship's Provisions
9. Fresh Water Tanks
10. Steam Turbine Engine
11. Kitchen, First and Second Class
12. Reciprocating (Piston) Steam Engines
13. Boilers
14. Kitchen, First Class
15. Coal Bunkers
16. Dining Saloon, First Class
17. Dining Saloon, Third Class
18. First Class Reception
19. Turkish Bath
20. Swimming Pool
21. Watertight Bulkhead (one of fifteen)
22. Mail Room
23. Squash Court
24. Motor Cars
25. Fire Fighter's Passage
26. Hull (double-bottom)
27. Porthole
28. Smoking Room, Third Class
29. Cranes
30. Second Class Entrance
31. Aftmast
32. Dining Saloon, Second Class

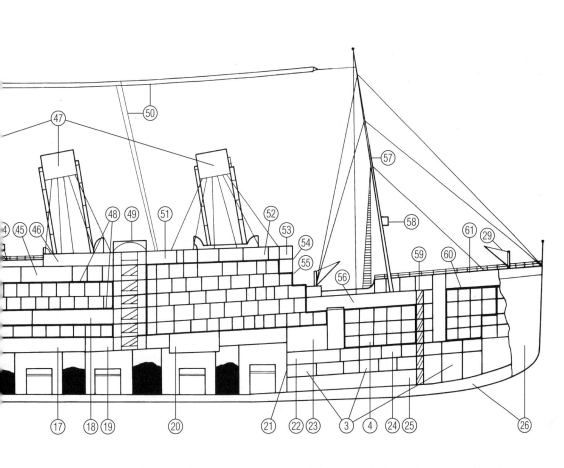

33. Smoking Room, Second Class
34. Library
35. Veranda Cafe
36. Bar
37. Restaurant
38. Dummy Smokestack
39. Smoking Room, First Class
40. Aft First Class Vestibule and Staircase
41. Aft State Rooms First Class
42. Maids' and Valets' Dining Saloon
43. Lounge
44. Compass Platform
45. Writing Room
46. Gymnasium
47. Smokestacks
48. Forward State Rooms, First Class

49. Forward First Class Grand Staircase
50. Marconi Antenna Wire
51. Marconi (Radio) Room
52. Officers' Quarters
53. Bridge
54. Boat Deck
55. Promenade Deck
56. Third Class Open Space
57. Foremast
58. Crow's Nest
59. Hatch Way
60. Crew's Quarters
61. Forecastle

This is a bedroom in one of the First Class suites onboard the Titanic. *No expense was spared in preparing the rooms that would accommodate some of the wealthiest people in the world.*

May 31, crowds of people began gathering at the shipyard. The steamer *Duke of Argyll* brought reporters and distinguished visitors from England, across the Irish Sea, for the grand event.

Throughout the morning other spectators arrived, aboard railway cars and boats. Thousands of men who had helped build the ship sat on stacks of timber to observe the launch. According to one eyewitness, these workers "greeted their handwork, dropped their tools, and raised their hoarse voices in a cheer. The miracle had happened."[5]

As chairman of Harland & Wolff, Lord Pirrie greeted the important guests and led them to festively draped observation stands, where they sat along the portside bow of the ship. The owners were grouped nearby. Pirrie had donned a yachting cap for the occasion, which was also the date of both his own and his wife's birthday.

The *Titanic*'s hull gleamed with a fresh coat of black paint. As the harbor was cleared of other craft, workers completed the final tasks that had to be done before

the enormous vessel could be slid down the ways into the water. These had been greased with fifteen tons of tallow, five tons of tallow mixed with locomotive oil, and three tons of soft soap. As the last timber supports were knocked loose, the spectators cheered and shouted, "There she goes!"[6] Shortly after 12:15, the ship was afloat.

After the launching, White Star hosted a gala luncheon for honored guests, including the engineers, naval architects, and port officials, at the Grand Central Hotel. The press attended a special event at the same hotel. Lord and Lady Pirrie hosted a smaller gathering at the shipyard for Mr. and Mrs. Ismay and J. P. Morgan. Later that afternoon, the Pirries joined the distinguished guests aboard the *Olympic*, which took them back from Belfast to England. The passengers admired the ship's lush interiors and its many innovations, including the first swimming pool on a ship.

Meanwhile, the *Titanic* was placed in a fitting-out berth, where its superstructure and the final work on it could be completed. Skilled workers laid electrical cables and air ducts throughout the ship. By January the four funnels, or smokestacks (one of which was for ventilation only), had been installed.

Completing the interior of the ship required several million hours of work over two months. The White Star Line gave the *Titanic* special features to distinguish her from the *Olympic*. Her staterooms were more opulent, paneled and furnished in different period styles: English Regency, Tudor, Louis XVI, and so on. Instead of portholes, these staterooms boasted windows with ocean views. Part of the promenade deck had a glass enclosure so that passengers could stroll in any kind of weather. First Class passengers would also enjoy a large, airy French-staffed restaurant designed to resemble the outdoor cafes of Paris.

In February 1912, the *Titanic* was placed in dry dock. The propellers were fitted and a final coat of paint was applied. On April 2, she was commissioned for brief sea trials.

"Practically Unsinkable"

Publicity about the ship swelled as the date of its maiden, or first, voyage drew near. It was discussed in scientific and shipping journals as well as the popular press. Companies that were providing supplies like soap, silverware, or bed linens for the ship proudly used the name "Titanic" in their advertising.

As descriptions and pictures of the *Titanic* circulated, public interest mounted. Movie audiences could see a newsreel that showed the exterior and interior of the finished ship. People were awed by its size and magnificent appointments.

The ship was hailed as a marvel of modern engineering, and its special safety features were noted. The *Titanic* had twenty-nine boilers, with every boiler compartment having its own pumping system. The ship's wireless had three potential sources of power: electric power from the engine room, backup current generated in another part of the ship, and storage batteries kept

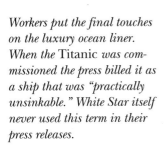

Workers put the final touches on the luxury ocean liner. When the Titanic *was commissioned the press billed it as a ship that was "practically unsinkable." White Star itself never used this term in their press releases.*

A Class-Conscious World

Life aboard the *Titanic* mirrored the class-conscious world of 1912. People then were more apt to be judged in terms of their family background, social status, and degree of wealth. People who lacked wealth or status tended to "know their place" and were more inclined to accept inequitable treatment as a fact of life.

In the United States, the very rich were the celebrities of their day. Unlike Europe, there were no American royal families. Actors and athletes were not as famous as they are today. Curious people followed the lavish parties, weddings, and other activities of rich Americans. The press reported their comings and goings and described their clothing, jewelry, homes, and yachts.

Author Robert D. Ballard in *Exploring the Titanic* has compared the *Titanic* to a "layer cake" with the layers of society traveling on different levels of the ship. Passengers stayed in their own specific areas, according to the price of their tickets, separated by gates and walls. First Class passengers enjoyed the best accommodations and service, including luxurious public rooms and walkways. Second Class and Third Class passengers were confined to smaller, less ornate parts of the ship. They were forbidden to enter the First Class areas.

The cost of passage varied dramatically. First Class passengers, most of whom were wealthy Americans, paid between $1,500 and $4,350 (more than $55,000 in current money) for their suites. In those days such an amount would have supported a British family comfortably for ten years. Second Class tickets cost $65 and up, depending on the size and quality of the room. Most Second Class passengers came from Britain. Tickets in Third Class (steerage) cost about $35. Passengers in the Third Class area of the *Titanic* were immigrants from Ireland, Italy, Syria, Armenia, China, Japan, Russia, Scandinavia, the Netherlands, and other countries. Their occupations, as listed on the ship's manifest, or passenger register, included bricklayer, baker, jeweler, shoemaker, tailor, miner, clerk, painter, servant, and tinsmith.

When they arrived in New York City, many new immigrants rented apartments in slum tenements, some of which were owned by the rich traveling on the *Titanic*'s upper decks. Low-paying jobs would keep many of these people poor throughout their working lives.

in the radio room. Although some members of the press called the ship "invincible" or "unsinkable," the White Star Line itself did not use these terms.

The public seemed ready to believe such claims, however. The recent decades had been marked by peace in the Western world and steady economic growth and technological progress. These conditions tended to give people feelings of security, trust, and optimism.

The captains and crews of the powerful modern ships also had developed great confidence in their vessels and felt more secure than they had aboard older ships. As a result, they became less worried and, perhaps, less vigilant.

Captain Edward Smith expressed such thoughts years before he took charge of the *Titanic*. In 1907 he told a newspaper reporter, "I cannot imagine any condition

Some of the First Class suites on the Titanic *cost $5,000 (Its modern day equivalent would be over $50,000). In 1912 that amount of money could have comfortably supported a British family for ten years.*

which would cause a ship to founder. . . . Modern shipbuilding has gone beyond that."[7] Author Geoffrey Marcus has pointed out the feeling that developed around the new ships, which "bred a false sense of security. . . . Risks were steadily increasing as ships became faster, larger, and proportionately weaker. . . . The risks they were running in 1912 were not the same risks that had been run in 1892; or even in 1902: but greater—very much greater."[8]

A Prestigious Ticket

In the highest social circles, people were judged not only by their family background, homes, friends, parties, and manner of dress, but also by the ships on which they traveled. Therefore, it was no surprise that fashionable travelers sought passage on the maiden voyage of the newest luxury liner, the *Titanic*. One passenger later described the mood at that time:

> The world had waited expectantly for its launching and again for its sailing; had read accounts of its tremendous size and unexampled completeness and luxury; had felt it a matter of the greatest satisfaction that such a comfortable, and above all such a safe boat had been designed and built—the unsinkable lifeboat.[9]

When would the *Titanic* sail? A coal strike throughout Britain that began in early spring caused numerous ships to cancel scheduled voyages. The boilers of the *Titanic* consumed a hefty 650 tons of coal every day, but the owners managed to acquire what they needed in time for the maiden voyage.

This poster announces the first and only voyage of the R.M.S. Titanic. *The ship would depart from Southampton, England, and make two stops before steaming across the Atlantic to New York.*

In the meantime, Thomas Andrews and his design department worked hard during the first week of April to prepare the great ship and her crew. He personally supervised much of the work, answering crew members' questions and demonstrating the various features of the ship. His secretary said that no job was too small for Andrews, who "put in their place such things as racks, tables, chairs, berth ladders, electric fans, saying that except he saw everything right he could not be satisfied."[10] To his wife, Andrews wrote, "The *Titanic* is now about complete."[11]

A Careful Inspection?

The White Star Line announced that the *Titanic* would indeed depart on April 10, 1912. From Southampton, England, the great ship would head for Cherbourg, France, then to Queenstown, Ireland, before steaming toward New York.

A few days before the sailing date, a Board of Trade inspector known to be a stickler for detail examined the ship. It was his job to make sure that all the proper equipment—lifeboats, lifejackets, emergency rockets, flares, and lights—was on board and in good working order. The *Titanic* passed his careful inspection and even surpassed some of the safety requirements. She was pronounced ready to go.

Chapter

2 All Aboard!

As day broke, the White Star Line's boat train arrived at the harbor of Southampton where the *Titanic* stood majestically in its slip. Before the voyage began, members of the press and the Second and Third Class passengers were allowed to view the magnificent First Class public rooms. They reported that these rooms were even more impressive than what they had been led to expect.

Residents of Southampton came to watch the historic departure and to bid farewell to crew members, many of whom lived in this seaside town. A newspaperman described the scene:

> The vision of the great liner as she moved away from Southampton quay forms an imperishable memory. She

looked so colossal and so queenly. Passengers waved farewells from her decks and windows, and a mob of jolly stokers yelled from the fo-castle side. One of these—he must have been a Cockney—played a mouth organ and waved his old cap. He seemed a merry soul.[12]

At noon the ship left port. Six tugboats guided the *Titanic* into the channel that led to the Test River and on to the Atlantic. The tugboats gone, she steamed down the channel under her own power to where two smaller liners, the *New York* and the *Oceanic,* were docked. As the *Titanic* passed the *New York,* the suction from the *Titanic's* propellers pulled the other ship loose from its moorings. For an instant it seemed certain that the two ships would collide.

The Titanic *steams out of Southampton toward Cherbourg, France. The ship was so large that it could not dock in Cherbourg. The passengers had to be ferried out to the luxury liner in smaller ships.*

Captain Edward Smith quickly ordered the crew to turn off one of the engines and to steer the *Titanic* away from the *New York*. At the same time, the captain of one of the tugboats, the *Vulcan*, passed a line to the stern of the *New York* to help pull the smaller ship back. With a crash narrowly averted, the *Titanic* moved out to sea as the *New York* was towed to a different berth.

In later years people would cite this near accident as a bad omen. There were also rumors that twenty-two men who had signed on as crew members did not show up, because they believed the *Titanic* was unlucky. Some of the crew also said they had heard that a mummy with a curse on it was stowed in the ship's cargo compartment. However, most of the crew laughed at such talk. They had been selected to work on the greatest ship ever built and they were proud and excited to be on board.

Endless Chores

As the ship steamed out of port, the crew members were hard at work throughout it. The White Star Line had assembled 892 top employees for this voyage, many of them transferred from the *Olympic* and other major liners.

In charge was Captain Edward J. Smith, who had been the master of the *Olympic*. It was said that Smith might retire after this voyage or perhaps after commanding the maiden voyage of the next great White Star liner, the *Gigantic*. A group of five officers, reporting directly to Smith, supervised the rest of the crew. Thirty-eight-year-old Henry Tighe Wilde, who had been Smith's chief officer on the *Olympic*, served in that same role on the *Titanic*.

The first officer was a Scotsman, William McMaster Murdoch, who had served in the Atlantic aboard the *Arabic, Adriatic, Oceanic,* and *Olympic*. Charles Herbert Lightoller was second officer. Like the others, he had gone to sea as a youth and had served in many posts on ships bound for Australia and other ports. Third Officer Herbert John Pitman, Fourth Officer Joseph Grove Boxhall, and Fifth Officer Harold Godfrey Lowe were likewise experienced, proven seamen.

Three hundred and forty men worked below decks for the engineering department, as engineers, electricians, trimmers, boilermakers, greasers, and firemen. Stokers shoveled vast quantities of coal into the ship's furnaces to run the steam engines that moved the propellers. Trimmers trundled wheelbarrows filled with coal from the bunkers to the furnaces, over and over again. The air in those rooms remained hot and thick with coal dust.

More than half the crew were assigned to care for the passengers and their accommodations. There were 390 stewards and stewardesses, along with numerous maids and deck workers. Nine men were assigned to polish the First Class passengers' shoes. Among the other crew members were a masseuse, a linen keeper, a window cleaner, a stenographer, an exercise instructor, a carpenter, a night watchman, and barbers.

Maritime historian John Maxtone-Graham describes the duties of a steward or stewardess assigned to cabin service:

[He or she] made beds, cleaned the cabin and, if there was one, its adjoining bathroom; . . . kept the alleyways vacuumed, swept and dusted; . . . brought trays for breakfast or tea (or, indeed, any meal requested), answered summonses, ran errands, arranged flowers, turned down beds at night, put away clothing, and, invariably, comforted and cosseted the seasick.[13]

Author Geoffrey Marcus gives a vivid picture of the work that took place between the engineering room and the top, or boat, deck:

The duty watch washing down decks and cleaning the paintwork, shifting and stacking chairs and cleaning up generally; T. W. McCawley, the white-flannelled gymnasium instructor, assisting people to ride the mechanical "horse" and "camel"; chefs and their underlings endlessly preparing dishes in the various galleys; the restaurant cashier busy with her accounts; the nurse on duty in the sick bay; library stewards filling in or cancelling slips as books were taken out or returned; page-boys hurrying on the track of errant passengers; the Purser's staff keeping the ship's books, receiving the reports of the stewards and cooks, and supervising the issue of the day's stores; lift-boys wafting passengers up and down between the different decks.[14]

Also at work on the *Titanic* were a printer and his assistants, an interpreter, a squash coach, mechanics, bath attendants, postal clerks, barmen, florists, and dozens of others.

Six lookouts were on board. Working in pairs, they kept watch at all times from the "crow's nest" located at the top of the bow, or the front, of the ship.

Two small all-male orchestras—one with five musicians, the other with three—were on hand to entertain passengers. The trio played in the Second Class dining room

The Titanic*'s captain, Edward J. Smith (right) was a well-respected seaman with over forty years of experience. Smith had noted that in all of his years at sea he had never been involved in an accident that resulted in a wreck.*

and lounge while the quintet, led by thirty-three-year-old violinist Wallace Hartley, performed for the First Class passengers during luncheon and dinner. These men also gave recitals in the lounge and strolled through the palm court playing the exuberant tunes that marked the era. In 1912, the most popular operettas, musical comedies, and dance tunes, especially American ragtime, were lighthearted. The musicians' repertoire came from the White Star songbook, which included 352 pieces all the musicians on board had to be able to play from memory.

A Select Gathering

When the *Titanic* left Southampton to pick up the rest of its passengers, it had a number of First Class passengers, most of the Second Class passengers, and a few who held Third Class tickets. Even the most sophisticated travelers, of whatever class,

J. Bruce Ismay (center), managing director of the White Star Line, and one of the Titanic*'s survivors, was eager to show the world that the* Titanic *was one of the finest ships ever built.*

sop and other crew members from the *Olympic* were happy to see Andrews, whom they regarded as being "a very humane gentleman." [15] While examining the *Olympic*, Andrews had taken time to ask the crew how he could improve the *Titanic*. Jessop was pleased to find that her bunk had been situated in a way that gave her more privacy and that she and her cabin mate had small, separate wardrobes, instead of having to share one. As she later wrote,

> It was quite unusual for members of the catering department [stewards and stewardesses] to be consulted about changes that would benefit their comforts or ease their toil. So when [Andrews] paid us this thoughtful compliment, we realized it was a great privilege; our esteem for him, already high, knew no bounds. [16]

The most prominent First Class passengers occupied luxurious paneled suites furnished with antiques, crystal chandeliers, and the finest linens. John Jacob Astor IV and his bride of eight months, the former Madeleine Force, were the wealthiest couple on board. Their marriage had caused a sensation in September 1911, coming as it had less than two years after Astor had divorced his first wife, Ava. After high society snubbed the couple, the forty-eight-year-old Astor took his nineteen-year-old bride abroad, hoping the matter would die down. Now Madeleine was pregnant and the Astors were going home. After boarding, they proceeded to the opulent rooms they had reserved on the *Titanic*, one of the two "millionaire's suites."

were impressed by the huge ship as they stepped off the gangplank and had their first views of the *Titanic*.

Two First Class passengers, Bruce Ismay and Thomas Andrews, were on board to evaluate the ship's performance. As managing director of the White Star Line, Ismay was eager to show the world that the *Titanic* was a superior vessel in every respect. At Southampton, he had shown the ship to his wife and children, who saw him off, then left for a trip of their own in England.

Thomas Andrews, who had supervised the design of the ship, was also on board. As usual, he set to work at once and spent his time aboard the *Titanic* inspecting even the smallest details of the ship and making recommendations. Stewardess Violet Jes-

Also on board were an older couple, Isidor and Ida Straus, who had spent the winter in southern France. Straus, a millionaire, was a former congressman who with his brother had helped build the famous Macy's department store in New York City and another store called Abraham & Straus. This unassuming couple was popular with the crew, who knew them from previous voyages on White Star ships.

Artists, writers, and fashion designers were among the other passengers. Theatrical producer Henry B. Harris and his wife, singer René Harris, were on board. Author Helen Churchill Candee had written an advice book called *How Women May Earn a Living* and numerous other books on various topics. Candee, traveling alone,

From Steerage to Millionaire's Suite: The Astors

In 1912 the Astors were the wealthiest family in America and one of the wealthiest in the world. Yet the founder of the family fortune had once traveled in the lowliest section of the ship that took him to the United States. In 1783, Jack Astor's great-grandfather, John Jacob Astor I, was a penniless twenty-year-old German emigrant. For a few dollars he bought a ticket in the steerage section of the *North Carolina*, bound for Baltimore. After an uncomfortable journey, the ship reached Chesapeake Bay, where the water froze, trapping several ships in the ice. For a week, the passengers had to wait for the ice to thaw.

Astor had brought along some flutes and clarinets made by his brother George, who owned a small musical instrument factory in London. After he disembarked, Astor sold these instruments in Baltimore and used the money to move to New York, where he developed a successful fur-trading business. With the profits from this business Astor bought real estate and ships to sail the routes between Europe and Asia. When he died in 1848 at age eighty-four, Astor's fortune was estimated at a then-staggering $20 million.

By the time John Jacob (Jack) Astor IV was born in 1864, his family owned entire streets in New York City, including thousands of rental properties. Some of these properties were tenement apartments that housed poor immigrants in the slum sections where people were crowded into dark, windowless rooms with no running water or heat. The Astors rented these buildings to other people, who in turn rented them to the poor. After the New York Tenement House Commission of 1894 investigated these buildings and issued a critical report, Jack Astor and his cousin William Waldorf decided to sell their buildings so they would no longer be reproached as "slum landlords."

soon became part of a congenial shipboard group that included Colonel Archibald Gracie, English sculptor Hugh Woolner, and American architect Edward A. Kent. The famous artist Francis David Millet and renowned engineer Washington Augustus Roebling, the chief designer of the Brooklyn Bridge, had elected to travel on the *Titanic*, as had two well-known American tennis players, Dick Williams and Karl Behr.

The English author Lawrence Beesley traveled Second Class, along with other middle-class people from Britain. As the

John Jacob Astor (seen with his wife, Madeleine) was one of the richest men in the world. He perished in the frigid waters of the North Atlantic along with 1,500 others. His wife survived and later bore his child.

voyage commenced, Beesley met the Reverend Ernest Carter and his wife Lilian; the three spent much of their time together talking about their education, work, and families. Other Second Class passengers included families with children, including twelve-year-old Ruth Becker, who was traveling with her mother and younger brother.

The ship crossed the English Channel and reached Cherbourg, France, on the first evening. There, the *Titanic* welcomed 142 First Class passengers, 30 Second Class travelers, and 102 Third Class passengers. The port in Cherbourg was not large enough for the *Titanic*, so the passengers and their baggage had to be carried out in smaller-sized boats called tenders. This process took a few hours.

Mrs. Charlotte Cardeza, a wealthy Philadelphian, came aboard in Cherbourg with fourteen trunks, four suitcases, and three crates. Among the contents were seventy gowns, ten fur coats, ninety-one pairs of gloves, and numerous other items. In those days many wealthy women took thousands of dollars' worth of jewels on transatlantic trips.

George Widener, a streetcar magnate from Philadelphia, boarded with his wife and their adult son, Harry, a well-known book collector. They occupied the other "millionaire's suite" on B Deck. Major Archibald Butt, a military aide to President William Howard Taft, was returning home after a vacation he had taken on the advice of his doctor and with the blessing of his friend the president. In a letter to his sister-in-law before the voyage, Butt wrote, "Don't forget that all my papers are in a storage warehouse, and if the old ship goes down you will find my affairs in shipshape condition."[17]

Seventeen-year-old John (Jack) Thayer Jr. and his parents were among the First Class passengers who boarded in Cherbourg. His father was a vice president of the Pennsylvania Railroad. The family was returning home to Philadelphia; in the meantime, they enjoyed a wood-paneled suite that contained marble sinks and large, comfortable beds.

Benjamin Guggenheim, an American millionaire whose Swiss ancestors had made a fortune in various commercial businesses, including the smelting industry, also boarded in Cherbourg, along with French author Jacques Futrelle. Other First Class passengers included William Ryerson, a steel magnate from Philadelphia, with his wife; Sir Cosmo and Lady (Lucile) Duff-Gordon; and Mrs. J. J. (Margaret, or Molly) Brown.

The wealthiest passengers brought their own servants to unpack their belongings and ensure their comfort. The thirty-one private maids, valets (manservants), and governesses on board the *Titanic* could spend their free time in a lounge set aside just for them.

There were three well-known cardsharps on the *Titanic*, all traveling under false names in pursuit of fortune. Other gamblers may also have been aboard but were not recognized. Professional cardsharps regularly crossed the Atlantic on luxury liners, where they made money gambling with wealthy passengers.

Well-to-do passengers on the *Titanic* did not have to leave their favorite pets behind. They were carefully tended to in a kennel on board. Among those who brought their dogs aboard was Jack Astor. Other passengers had purchased pets during their European travels. Wealthy travelers also brought sports equipment and even new cars on board.

Isidor Straus, a New York merchant and former congressman, was one of the many well-to-do passengers on the Titanic. *When he was offered a place in a lifeboat with his wife, he declined. His wife got out of the boat and joined her husband on the deck.*

Last Stop

Before heading out from Cherbourg toward the Irish coast, Captain Smith took extra time to familiarize himself with his new ship. Under his direction the crew practiced a few turns in the water, after which the *Titanic* headed to Queenstown, Ireland, to board the last group of passengers.

On the morning of Thursday, April 11, luncheon was being served as the ship anchored off Roche's Point, Ireland. Tenders brought the new passengers and mail out from Queenstown. More than one hundred Irish emigrants came on board, along with vendors displaying fine handmade lace, Irish linens, and other wares. Jack

The Millionaire's Captain

Captain Edward J. Smith, known affectionately as E. J., had been at sea for more than forty years when he was asked to take command of the *Titanic*. In 1869, Smith had begun his career on a clipper ship as a seventeen-year-old apprentice. He learned his way around a ship by serving in numerous positions and then as a commander with the British Royal Naval Reserve during the Boer War at the turn of the century.

In 1880, Smith joined the White Star Line as fourth officer on the *Celtic*. Seven years later he had worked his way up the ranks to become a captain. Smith was so highly regarded that the White Star Line assigned him to the *Olympic* when it was put into service in 1911. By 1912 he had commanded seventeen vessels for the company and was receiving a salary of £1,250 a year. The captains of other liners usually earned less, some just £300 per year.

A number of wealthy passengers were in the habit of booking passage on his ships because they liked and respected Captain Smith. The fifty-nine-year-old skipper was regarded as a calm, fair-minded person who maintained good discipline on his ships and inspired confidence. Passengers as well as crew members praised his warm personality and management skills. Standing on the bridge in his navy-blue uniform with its stiff collar and four rings denoting his seniority on each sleeve, Smith was an imposing figure.

Author Walter Lord quotes from an interview Smith gave to the press in 1907 when he took over a new ship, the *Adriatic*:

> When anyone asks me how I can best describe my experiences of nearly forty years at sea, I merely say "uneventful." I have never seen an accident of any sort worth speaking about. I never saw a wreck and have never been wrecked, nor was I ever in any predicament that threatened to end in disaster of any sort.

When the White Star Line's officials assigned Smith to the *Titanic*, they said they had "absolute confidence" in his ability.

Astor bought his wife a lace shawl for $800.

By now there were thirteen honeymooning couples on board, from Virginia, New York, and other states, including one couple from Spain. Several large families were traveling together as emigrants. Alma and

William Skoog and their four children hailed from Norway. A British couple, Fred and Augusta Goodwin, had their six children, and John and Annie Sage of England came aboard with nine. Irish emigrant Margaret Rice and her five sons—Albert, George, Eric, Arthur, and Eugene—were also on board. (All these people died when the ship went down.)

The *Titanic* left port in Ireland at 1:30 P.M. on April 11, scheduled to reach New York City the following Wednesday morning. The official tally was 1,316 passengers and 892 crew members, but there may have been even more on board. The official numbers were based on ticket sales and the crew lists, but stowaways may have come aboard, and a few passengers on the list may have failed to make the trip. In all, counting passengers and crew, the ship carried about 60 percent of her capacity, since she could accommodate 905 passengers in First Class, 564 in Second Class, 1,134 in Third Class (for a total of 2,603) and 944 crew members.

Cancelled Plans

A number of people who planned to travel on the *Titanic* either did not show up or cancelled their plans. Some of them simply missed the boat. A group of men who had signed up as crew members lingered in a Southampton tavern too long and arrived at the docks late for duty. They were told that their jobs had been filled and were ordered to leave. An American, Frank Carlson, had hoped to board the *Titanic* at Cherbourg, but his car broke down while he was driving to that city, so he did not make the trip.

For various reasons, fifty-five passengers cancelled their reservations on the *Titanic*. Some withdrew because of illness or poor health. One couple cancelled because the man's mother disliked maiden voyages and pressured them to change their plans. In another case, a couple cancelled because the woman had a bad dream that the ship would sink.

"Firm as a Rock"

As more and more steam reached its engines, the *Titanic* gathered speed. She moved out to sea at a fast pace for 1912, about 21 knots. One knot—which measures 6,076 feet, or slightly more than one mile on land—is one nautical mile per

R. N. Williams (left) and Karl Behr, both professional tennis players, survived the Titanic *disaster. Williams, after recovering from severe frostbite, went on to win the U.S. Men's Singles Title in 1914, 1915, and 1916.*

This is the children's playground on the saloon deck of the Titanic. *There were over 110 children on the ship when it set sail in April of 1912.*

hour. The fastest ships operating in the late twentieth century do not travel much faster than the *Titanic.*

The mountains along the southern Irish coast faded into the distance as the ship moved away. In farewell, Third Class passenger Eugene Daly stood on deck playing the sorrowful song "Erin's Lament" on his bagpipes. Tearful emigrants took one last look at their homeland as the ship swept proudly out to sea, her name glittering in gold letters on the bow.

From Queenstown, Mrs. J. H. Loring sent a letter to friends. She praised the great ship and its appointments, ending with these words: "This is a huge ship and I think will be most comfortable."[18] The passengers were amazed that they could hardly hear the engines or feel any vibrations. Journalist W. T. Stead wrote to his wife, "The ship is firm as a rock and the sea is like a millpond."[19]

Chapter

3 "Nothing to Mar Our Pleasure"

The maiden voyage of the *Titanic* began smoothly. The passengers felt little rolling or vibration from the ship's engines, so very few of them were seasick. As the *Titanic* moved westward, most of the passengers enjoyed the fair weather and the sheer pleasure of being on board such a beautiful, efficiently run ship. Many of them located old friends and acquaintances aboard, and others were pleased to find congenial new companions.

One of the passengers, Mahala (Mrs. Walter D.) Douglas of Minneapolis, later described those first days aboard:

> Once off, everything seemed to go perfectly. The boat was so luxurious, so steady, so immense, and such a marvel of mechanism that one could not believe he was on a boat—and there the danger lay. We had smooth seas, clear, starlit nights, fresh favoring winds; nothing to mar our pleasure.[20]

Dr. Washington Dodge echoed these sentiments, saying,

> The weather was fine and the sea calm. At all times one might walk the decks, with the same security as if walking down Market Street, so little motion was there to the vessel. It was hard to realize, when dining in the large spa-

cious dining saloon, that one was not in some large and sumptuous hotel.[21]

A Floating Hotel

For the passengers a new day aboard the *Titanic* began with a bugle call signaling breakfast. Soon, stewards arrived with fresh copies of the *Atlantic Daily Bulletin*, the White Star Line's newspaper, printed on board. Then it was off to breakfast for those who wished to dine in the public rooms.

Passengers gather on the Titanic's *deck to enjoy the fair weather and smooth seas that marked the beginning of their ill-fated voyage.*

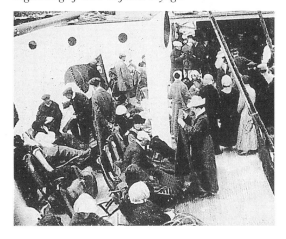

The Promenade deck of the Titanic. *Even with the help of printed maps and guides, most people, including some of the crew, found it difficult to get around without getting lost.*

Many of the passengers spent their first days on board touring the great ship and learning their way around. Even with the help of printed maps and guides, people found it difficult to sort out the labyrinth of long decks and passageways. The crew themselves were dazzled by the size of the ship. Second Officer Lightoller, known to his friends as "Lights," later said that

> it is difficult to convey the size of a ship like the *Titanic* where you could actually walk miles along decks and passages covering different ground all the time. . . . It took me fourteen days before I could with confidence find my way from one part of the ship to another.[22]

Most of the space on the *Titanic* was devoted to staterooms and public rooms for the First Class passengers, located primarily in the middle and upper decks. The staterooms on B Deck, for instance, boasted real windows instead of mere portholes. First Class passengers could also stroll along a private promenade deck that was shielded from cold winds by a glass dome.

Three of the four wood-paneled elevators were available to First Class passengers, and the fourth served Second Class.

The First Class public rooms resembled the parlors of grand hotels, with thick velvety carpets, downy sofas, and plush chairs. The finishing touches included crystal light fixtures, gilded mirrors, fine artwork, floral arrangements, and live plants.

There was much to admire throughout the ship. With its painted glass windows of landscapes, ships, and historical scenes and its comfortable leather chairs, the First Class smoking room offered male passengers a stylish retreat like the clubs they were used to frequenting at home. The Parisian-style cafe on B Deck was both elegant and inviting, its walls adorned with trellises and climbing leaves. A less formal veranda cafe contained red and brown cushioned wicker furniture. The First Class reading room, densely carpeted in dusty rose, with complementary pink draperies on the windows, contained numerous books and current magazines. A fine oil painting called "Plymouth Harbour" hung over the marble fireplace.

A major attraction in First Class was the grand staircase leading into the dining saloon, located on D Deck, with an adjoining reception room. An elaborate dome of leaded glass covered the finely carved staircase. Two sets of steps paused at a paneled landing, then descended on both sides. On the wall of the landing a beautiful clock was mounted surrounded by ornate carvings.

The white-walled Jacobean-style reception room at the bottom of the grand staircase held airy wicker furniture and potted palms. From there passengers entered the dining saloon, which was as wide as the *Titanic* itself and could hold more than five hundred people. Alcoves along the sides were available for those who wished to dine more privately.

The First Class passengers could also dine in the À La Carte restaurant, with its outdoor Café Parisien, unique to the *Titanic.* This restaurant gave passengers more choices, allowing them to order food from a diverse menu from 8:00 A.M. through 11:00 P.M. Meals here cost extra, because the restaurant was a private concession operated by a London restaurateur, Luigi Gattie.

An indoor swimming pool—unusual in ships at the time—and squash courts were added attractions. They were located on the lower decks, as was the Turkish bath, adorned with blue-green tiles, a red and gold ceiling, and teakwood columns. A gymnasium on the uppermost deck featured exercise equipment including stationary bicycles and rowing machines. An English gym instructor, T. W. McCawley, was on hand to demonstrate the machines and encourage people to try them.

Passengers on the *Titanic* also enjoyed browsing in the two barbershops, one for

The long journey across the Atlantic started very smoothly for the Titanic. *The vessel was so large and opulently furnished that passengers often forgot they were on an ocean-going vessel.*

First Class men, the other for Second Class. Besides haircuts and shaves, the shops offered postcards, gifts, and souvenirs.

Second Class Luxury

Toward the stern of the *Titanic*, and also on the upper decks, were the Second Class cabins. These rooms, which occupied the smallest portion of the ship, were attractively and simply furnished. Located on D, E, and F Decks, the Second Class cabins had white paneling, linoleum floors, and mahogany furnishings. The corridors leading to these staterooms were carpeted in red or green.

The Second Class travelers could stroll on their own promenade deck, located on the port (left) side of their section of the ship. These passengers also had a smoking room (aft on B Deck) and a library (on C Deck). Their smoking room was paneled in oak and furnished with oak pieces upholstered in dark green leather. The brown-carpeted library had sycamore paneling and mahogany furnishings, complemented with tapestry upholstery and green silk draperies. Enclosed promenades were on either side.

Forty Tons of Potatoes

Preparing and serving top-quality meals and refreshments aboard the *Titanic* required a large, talented staff of chefs, waiters, and busboys. The kitchen staff included chefs, soup cooks, a fish cook, a roast cook, vegetable cooks, and several bakers. Twelve thousand dinner plates were needed for the three classes of passengers.

Immense quantities of food were stored in the ship's pantries, refrigerators, and freezers. Among other things, the *Titanic* carried 40,000 eggs, 75,000 pounds of fresh meat, 11,000 pounds of fresh fish, 7,500 pounds of ham and bacon, 36,000 oranges, 1,000 pounds of grapes, 6,000 pounds of butter, 7,000 heads of lettuce, 2¾ tons of tomatoes, 40 tons of potatoes, 2,250 pounds of fresh peas, 1,750 quarts of ice cream, and 10,000 pounds of sugar.

The *Titanic*'s kitchens were equipped with the most up-to-date machines and appliances. Passengers heard so much about these kitchens that they asked to tour these areas of the ship. There they saw for themselves the huge refrigerators and the various devices the staff used to chop, slice, and peel foods that later appeared in such dishes as mushroom consommé, omelettes seasoned with herbs, filet of sole in wine sauce, soufflé potatoes, and compotes of fruit.

The Second Class public rooms on the *Titanic* were as luxurious as the First Class public rooms to be found on other liners. Ruth Becker, a twelve-year-old traveling with her mother and brother, was impressed by the sparkling freshness of everything on the ship. As she later wrote, "Everything was new. New! Our cabin was just like a hotel room, it was so big. The dining room was beautiful—the linens, all the bright polished silver you can imagine."[23]

Third Class Comfort

Likewise, Third Class quarters on the *Titanic* were the most comfortable available on any steam liner of the day. Placed in the lowest parts of the ship, these steerage rooms were small but clean, supplied with bunks, a washbasin, and good heating and lighting. They were paneled in pine and finished with simple floor coverings.

The Third Class passengers had public rooms, too, another unique feature of the *Titanic*. For many passengers these rooms were larger and more comfortable than those in their own homes. Men could socialize in two bars or the smoking room. Next to that room was a general room, or passenger lounge, paneled in pine and finished in white enamel, with tables, chairs, and benches made of teakwood. The room also contained a piano, one of sixteen carried on the ship. In the Third Class dining room, meals were plain but ample and well prepared, again often better than what the passengers typically ate at home.

Various European languages could be heard in the steerage section of the ship. Herr Hoffman, an interpreter, was on board to help passengers communicate, but most

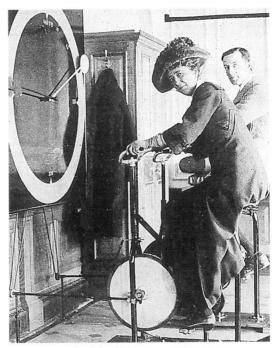

The Titanic *had a gymnasium that was fully furnished with the latest exercise equipment and a physical fitness instructor to show people how to use it. Here two passengers make use of the stationary bikes.*

Third Class travelers tended to congregate with people of their own nationality.

Evenings in the steerage section were festive as people milled around the public rooms, singing, dancing, and talking, while children played. Standing on the Third Class promenade deck at the stern of the ship, these passengers could gaze at the star-filled sky and the expanse of white foam the powerful ship left in its wake.

Pleasant Hours

Except for mealtimes, passengers on the *Titanic* had no set schedule. Breakfast was served between 8:30 and 10:30 A.M., luncheon between 1:00 and 2:30 P.M., and dinner between 6:00 and 7:30 P.M. or slightly later. During the rest of the day, people could do as they wished.

Passengers were free to enjoy the many natural wonders around them as they crossed the Atlantic: the scent of the sea air, miles of blue-green water, the changing skies. Second Class passenger Lawrence Beesley described one exquisite sunrise: "Each morning the sun rose behind us in a sky of circular clouds, stretching round the horizon in long, narrow streaks, and rising tier upon tier above the skyline, red and pink and fading from pink to white, as the sun rose higher in the sky."[24] Evening brought other wonders as vivid sunsets tinted the sky. Seemingly endless stars gleamed at night.

On the third day out, many passengers spent hours sitting on deck chairs, resting, reading, writing letters, or chatting. Stewards circulated with trays of steaming tea and broth, buttered toast, sandwiches, and fancy cakes. Children played under the watchful eyes of adults on the decks or in the enclosed promenades and stairways.

Dinner was a high point. The First Class dining room was resplendent with fine china and silver. Fastidiously groomed

The passengers onboard the Titanic *spent many hours socializing, writing letters and relaxing on the ship's many decks.*

"A Lucky Thing"

On her maiden voyage the *Titanic* contained the most up-to-date wireless equipment. In this respect she surpassed the safety regulations, because the capacity to send and receive telegrams—called Marconigrams, after their inventor, Guglielmo Marconi—was not required in ships at that time.

Telegraphy had made great strides since 1843 when the first electric telegraph was laid along the Great Western Railway in Britain. During the mid-1800s, messages traveled along cables. Then a long cable was laid across the Atlantic in 1865. Alexander Graham Bell found a way to transmit sound along wires, and the German physicist Heinrich Hertz was able to generate radio waves using electrical discharges. These developments laid the basis for the telegraph. The term *telegraph* was coined in 1792 when a Frenchman named Claude Chappe devised an upright semaphore post with movable arms that sent messages using a code.

In 1894, Marconi invented the "wireless." This talented twenty-two-year-old native of Italy then moved to London, where he could demonstrate and publicize his amazing device. In 1898 the British royal yacht became the first ship to use Marconi's wireless telegraph. Three years later, wireless signals were sent across the Atlantic. By 1912, when the *Titanic* sailed, hundreds of ships were using Marconi's device.

John G. Phillips and Harold S. Bride operated the *Titanic*'s wireless. Both men had been trained at the Marconi school in Liverpool, England, and were experienced telegraphers.

Bride, a survivor, later said it was "a lucky thing" the wireless was working at all the night the *Titanic* struck ice, because it had broken down that morning. He told a reporter for the *New York Times* that "we noticed something wrong on Sunday and Phillips and I worked seven hours to find it. We found a 'secretary' burned out, at last, and repaired it just a few hours before the iceberg was struck."

men appeared in white tie and tails or tuxedoes. The women sparkled with glamorous jewels and gowns, many of which they had just bought from top couturiers in Paris.

The five-piece orchestra played during dinner and, later, on the promenade as passengers enjoyed a walk or sat sipping coffee and liqueurs in the palm court. Lively conversations ensued in the smoking

After dinner was served, many passengers strolled the decks of the Titanic *dressed in the finest Paris fashions and jewels.*

room, where men congregated after dinner with their cigars and decks of cards or reading material.

While some passengers kept to themselves, many relished the social aspects of steamship travel. At the start of the voyage, a passenger list, printed in booklet form, was circulated so that people could discover who was on board. Since many of the wealthier passengers moved in the same social circles, they were already acquainted and some were close friends.

On Schedule

While the passengers dined, strolled, and socialized, the crew remained busy night and day. The engineering department worked especially hard as the ship increased its engine power and began traveling faster. The officers noted that the ship was behaving admirably at the higher speeds and was making excellent progress. Between noon Thursday and noon Friday, April 12, the ship logged 386 miles.

Around sunset Friday evening, the *Titanic* received a message from the steamer *La Touraine*. The wireless operators of that ship said that the *La Touraine* had encountered ice in nearby waters. The message did not seem to affect any decisions aboard the *Titanic*, which continued to increase its speed. During the next twenty-four hours, the *Titanic* covered 519 miles. The passengers were able to observe that the ship was moving faster. At this rate, they thought, they might even arrive in New York earlier than they had anticipated.

Chapter

4 Warning!

For three days and nights, the wireless operators on the *Titanic* were kept extremely busy sending and receiving messages. The passengers delighted in the novelty of exchanging personal greetings with friends and relatives on shore or on other ships. In addition, the wireless operators had to take down numerous other coded messages, for example, stock market quotations from New York, London, and Paris, and current events information, sent from Cape Cod, that would be used to compose the ship's newspaper.

On Sunday morning, April 14, the *Titanic* received another iceberg warning. It arrived at 9:00 A.M. and was directed to Captain E. J. Smith. The captain of the *Caronia*, another White Star ship, reported icebergs and pack ice—"bergs, growlers, and field ice"[25]—in an area that lay ahead of the *Titanic*. He identified the specific location of this ice. Chief Operator John G. Phillips handed the message to his assistant, asking Harold Bride to take it to Captain Smith on the bridge. The captain posted this message so that other crew members could also read it.

Meanwhile, the crew was preparing for the first Sunday on the *Titanic*. Workers had scraped and sanded the decks, and the public areas had been swept, mopped, dusted, and polished. Chief Engineer Joseph

Bell was at work directing the men who kept the boilers running. Kitchen workers hastened to prepare eggs, ham, bacon, sliced fruit, and different kinds of bread, including cornbread, which was popular with the Americans on board.

As usual on Sunday, the captain's inspection was held. A line of officers and department heads, led by Captain Smith, examined the ship from stem to stern and from top to bottom. Some of the passengers came out to see the line of smartly uniformed crew as they made their way through the *Titanic*.

A lifeboat drill was also customarily held before lunch on Sunday, but for some reason Captain Smith decided against it.

The radio room of the Titanic. *The wireless operators worked tirelessly for three days transmitting personal messages for the ship's guests.*

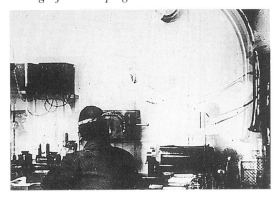

Perhaps he believed the passengers on his great ship would never need lifeboat preparation. Or he may have been reluctant for the passengers to see that there were not enough lifeboats for everyone on board.

At 10:30 A.M., Captain Smith led a religious service in the First Class dining saloon, including prayers and psalm readings. In the Second Class saloon Assistant Purser Reginald Barker conducted a service that ended with hymn number 418, "O God our help in ages past." A Catholic priest conducted mass, first in the Second Class lounge and then in steerage.

People proceeded to various activities, then luncheon. A major topic of conversation was the rate at which the ship was traveling. One passenger, Col. Archibald Gracie, later wrote that "in the twenty-four hours' run ending the 14th, according to [a posted notice], the ship had covered 546 miles, and we were told that the next twenty-four hours would see even a better record made." [26] Passengers discussed how far the *Titanic* had traveled from noon on Saturday to noon on Sunday. The news spread that the engines were now turning faster than they had since the voyage began. Those who had entered the daily sweepstakes to guess how many miles the ship had covered that day learned the results at noon in the smoking room.

Like the other passengers, those in the Second Class dining room speculated about when the ship would reach New York as they dined on consommé Fermier, cock-a-leekie, filets of brill, eggs à l'Argenteuil, chicken à la Maryland, corned beef, and vegetable dumplings. There were also grilled mutton chops and a choice of mashed, fried, or baked potatoes, as well as custard, apple meringue, and pastry.

By early afternoon the radio room had received two more warning messages, one from a Dutch liner, the *Noordam*, reporting "much ice" and another from the White Star liner *Baltic*, describing "icebergs and large quantities of field ice." [27]

The passengers were not privy to these warnings. As the day continued, they enjoyed another day of good weather and smooth traveling. Many of them chose to read or write letters. Athletically inclined people swam in the pool, used the exercise machines, or played squash and deck games like shuffleboard. However, a number of the passengers noticed that the air was growing colder. The crew also noticed the chill in the air and a drop in the water temperature, which was monitored on a regular basis. Archibald Gracie recalled that

towards evening the report, which I heard, was spread that wireless messages from passing steamers had been received advising the officers of our ship of the presence of icebergs and icefloes. The increasing cold and the necessity of being more warmly clad when appearing on deck were outward and visible signs in corroboration of these warnings. [28]

Full Speed Ahead

That evening, as usual, a bugle announced that it was time to dress for dinner. Several prominent First Class passengers assembled in the À La Carte restaurant, where Mr. and Mrs. George Widener were giving a dinner in honor of Captain Smith. Others enjoyed the main dining room on D Deck, where the entrée that evening was filet mignon.

Passengers enjoy the view and the fair weather on one of the Titanic*'s decks. None suspected that danger lay ahead of them in the ice-filled waters of the North Atlantic.*

Afterward, people gathered in the reception room and the palm court to sip coffee and hear classical music. Because it was Sunday, no dancing was permitted. Instead, a hymn sing was held in the dining room after dinner. A concert was given in the Second Class lounge, but the Third Class passengers had to create their own music.

Design engineer Thomas Andrews sat in the smoking room after dinner. He talked about the *Titanic* and his impressions of her so far, telling one passenger, "I believe her to be as nearly perfect as human brains can make her." [29]

Mrs. Walter D. Douglas of Minneapolis later described that last day on the ship:

On Sunday we had a delightful day; everyone in the best of spirits; the time the boat was making was considered very good, and all were interested in getting into New York early. . . . The evening was passed very quietly. As we went to our stateroom . . . we both remarked that the boat was going faster than she ever had. The vibration as one passed the stairway in the center was very noticeable." [30]

Treacherous Ice

Three more warnings would arrive that evening, all indicating a treacherous field of ice in the path of the great ship. Captain Smith saw at least four of the seven warnings that came throughout the day. Bruce Ismay was seen to read one of them, a message from the *Baltic* for Smith, then put it in his pocket.

Around 7:30 P.M., Harold Bride took a message from the *Californian* advising other ships in the vicinity that three large icebergs lay nearby. The operators gave the position of the ice, which lay about fifty miles ahead of the *Titanic* at that time. Bride delivered this message to Fourth Officer Joseph Boxhall, who was on navigation watch, and other crew members in the bridge. Captain Smith was still at dinner. The captain had authorized an increase in speed, to twenty-two and a half knots, despite the ice warnings that had been received throughout the day.

Smith returned to his command post around 9:00 P.M. and talked with Second Officer Herbert Lightoller, who was then

Floating Hazards

Icebergs are common in the North Atlantic during springtime. They arise in the northern glacier field off the coast of Greenland. As spring temperatures rise in the region, they melt and break off into large blocks of sea ice. Icebergs of different sizes then float offshore into the sea, along the western shore of Greenland and past eastern Canada and Newfoundland.

Thousands of icebergs break off each year, most of them coming from the west coast of Greenland. From there, a thousand or more reach the shipping lanes annually. (In 1972, the International Ice Patrol would count 1,587.)

In the northern shipping routes used in 1912, the number of icebergs often peaked during mid-April. Experienced captains and crews knew that they might well encounter ice in April, and some seamen said they could actually smell it when it was nearby. During the voyage of the *Titanic*, icebergs had drifted farther south than usual. The preceding winter had been warmer than normal, so more melting had occurred.

Icebergs can be immense, and rock hard. Growlers are small icebergs with only about three feet of them visible above the surface of the sea, yet they can weigh up to 100 tons. Large bergs can weigh as much as 1.5 million tons. They also often have sharp, rigid protrusions, as was true of the iceberg that the *Titanic* hit.

Several factors worked against the ship that night. The sea was calm and there was no moon. In a rough sea, waves foam up around the bases of the bergs, making them more visible. Moonlight would also have increased the chances of spotting the berg sooner.

Second Officer Lightoller later said that the side of the iceberg was dark. More than likely, this iceberg had turned over in the sea one or two hours before the collision. The small portion visible above the ocean's surface would have been dark because of containing water. Such icebergs are even more difficult to see until the water drains out, bringing back their usual white color.

on the bridge. Smith urged the crew to keep a close watch for icebergs. As he left to go to his cabin to sleep, Smith also warned Lightoller to beware of the slightest haziness in the air, saying, "If it becomes at all doubtful let me know at once. I will be just inside."[31]

Lightoller passed this order on to the other officers and seamen on duty. He told them to watch carefully for ice, especially smaller bergs. The new shift was given the same admonition when they came on duty.

Yet another ice warning came, from the cargo ship *Mesaba*, at 9:40 that evening. It reported "much heavy pack ice and great number large icebergs. Also field ice."[32] Radio operator Phillips was so busy he did not do anything with this message. The captain never saw it.

Frederick Fleet, the lookout who spotted the fatal iceberg, was one of the few crewmembers to survive the disaster.

Calm and Bright

The sea was calm that night. The passengers would later describe it as unusually calm, with brilliant stars filling the sky. When stewardess Violet Jessop went on deck before retiring, as was her custom, she found the air quite cold. She later wrote:

> Little wisps of mist like tiny fairies wafted gently inboard from the sea and left my face clammy. I shivered. It was indeed a night for bed, warmth and cozy thoughts of home and firesides. I thought of the men in the crow's nest as I came indoors, surely an unenviable job on such a night.[33]

When First Officer William Murdoch arrived at 10:00 P.M. to take over the watch from Lightoller, he remarked that it was very cold. Among other things, the two seamen discussed the problems of spotting icebergs on a calm night. Before leaving the bridge, Lightoller told Murdoch that the ship might come up to ice soon and that the captain had asked to be awakened should any difficulties arise.

Neither of these men saw the warning from the *Mesaba*, which would have told them where the ice lay. Nor had the men on lookout been informed of that message. At that time, Reginald Lee and Frederick Fleet were ascending the iron ladder into the lookout cage, the "crow's nest," relieving the men who had been on duty.

Later it appeared that the whole group of messages had never been read by one person or analyzed carefully to give the ship's officers, navigators, and lookouts a clear idea of what lay ahead. At the time, wireless operators had great discretion in deciding what to do with messages that came in not addressed to the captain or

The wireless operator on the Titanic, *Jack Phillips, was kept so busy relaying passengers' personal messages that he didn't relay the warning sent by the icebound* Californian *to the crew.*

another specific person. Captain Smith had posted only one incoming message, the 9:00 A.M. one from the *Caronia*.

The temperature fell steadily. At 10:30 P.M. the freighter *Rappahannock* signaled the *Titanic* as it passed the White Star ship that pack ice had damaged the bow and rudder of the *Rappahannock*. Using its Morse lamp, a crew member on the freighter signaled from its deck the message "Have just passed through heavy field ice and several icebergs."[34] The *Titanic* blinked back an acknowledgment.

By 11:00 P.M., the two radio operators were exhausted from long hours of unrelenting work. Bride paused for a nap while Phillips continued to transmit passenger messages that had accumulated.

Then a seventh ice warning came from the ship *Californian*, saying, "We're stopped and surrounded by ice." It was a loud signal that seemed to come from nearby. An overworked Phillips sputtered, "Shut up, shut up. I am busy."[35] The other operator stood by waiting for a response from the *Titanic* but at about 11:30 that operator, who was working alone on that ship, gave up and turned off his wireless and got ready for bed. The two ships were now no longer in contact.

By this time, most of the passengers on the *Titanic* had gone to bed too. The upper decks had become uncomfortably cold, even with the benefit of hot drinks and blankets. Several men remained awake in the smoking room playing bridge while others sat talking or reading in the leather chairs.

"Iceberg Right Ahead"

Up in the crow's nest, lookout Fred Fleet shivered and carefully kept his gaze ahead of the ship. A haze had momentarily passed by on the horizon in front of the *Titanic*, making his job more difficult. Suddenly, Fleet spotted a dark mass through the mist. He grabbed the brass alarm bell above the lookout and pulled sharply on its cord three times, then reached for the telephone.

The duty officer on the bridge, James Moody, came on the line. "Iceberg right ahead,"[36] Fleet told him. Moving swiftly through the water at at least 21 knots, the *Titanic* was coming closer and closer to the jagged iceberg every second.

Officer Murdoch, in charge of navigating during his watch, now faced a crisis. He ordered the crew to turn the wheel "hard a-starboard"—as far right as possible—while telling the men in the engine room to stop and reverse the engines. At once he rang the watertight door alarm to alert the men in the boiler rooms and reached for the switch that closed the doors to the compartments in the ship.

The crew waited grimly as the enormous ship slowly turned and avoided a head-on collision. It took four minutes to bring the ship to a complete halt, during which time the *Titanic* traveled nearly half a mile. The ship took longer to stop than it had taken to turn it. If the engines had not been turned off and then reversed, the *Titanic* would actually have turned faster.

A number of crew members were relieved to see the bow of the ship clear the iceberg. However, the part of the iceberg below the surface struck the ship's starboard bow. The ship hit the iceberg at 11:40 P.M. The collision itself was brief—only about ten seconds—but devastating. A sharp, hard projection from the iceberg jabbed the side of the hull for about three

hundred feet as the ship passed by. It created a series of holes and loosened rivets, penetrating the first three holds and boiler room number six. Seawater flowed into the lower compartments, despite the fact that the doors dividing them had been shut. Within minutes, the first three holds contained about fourteen feet of water.

Damage Below

The exact nature and extent of the problem was not immediately known at the time of the collision. The length of the gash allowed five compartments to flood. Because E, D, and C Decks ran together, had only the first four bulkheads filled with water, the flooding would not have risen above D Deck. But when a fifth

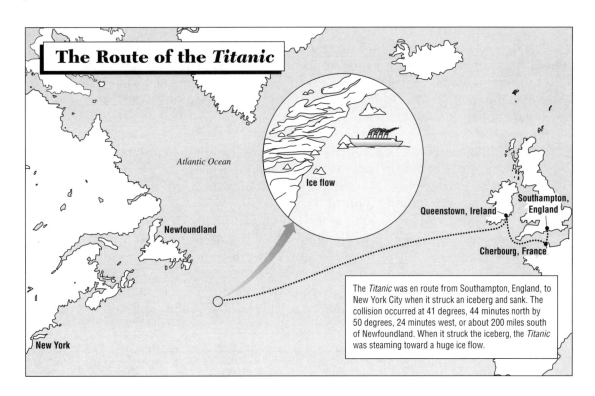

The Route of the *Titanic*

Atlantic Ocean

Ice flow

Newfoundland

Queenstown, Ireland

Southampton, England

Cherbourg, France

New York

The *Titanic* was en route from Southampton, England, to New York City when it struck an iceberg and sank. The collision occurred at 41 degrees, 44 minutes north by 50 degrees, 24 minutes west, or about 200 miles south of Newfoundland. When it struck the iceberg, the *Titanic* was steaming toward a huge ice flow.

compartment—boiler room six—flooded, this allowed water to spill over E Deck. It then flowed across the deck into the sixth compartment. The weight of this water then pulled down the bow of the ship.

The impact had knocked several tons of ice loose from the berg and onto the *Titanic*'s lower decks on her starboard side. Some people on the lower decks heard the noise and left their staterooms. They saw ice

"A . . . sort of shock"

At the time of the collision, the passengers and crew either heard and felt different sensations—or nothing at all, depending on where they were in the ship. Some passengers remained asleep, having heard and felt nothing. Others noticed a slight movement or heard scraping or grinding. Passengers on the upper decks did not know that an iceberg had struck the lower part of the hull, causing damage more severe than anything the builders of the *Titanic* had envisioned.

Some people on board felt a slight jarring sensation and heard a noise. Second Class passenger Kate Buss, who was awake reading, heard a noise that reminded her of a skate scraping on ice. In the smoking room just above Deck A people felt a jolt. Hugh Woolner would later describe that moment to a friend, writing, "There came a heavy grinding sort of a shock, beginning far ahead of us in the bows and rapidly passing along the ship and away under our feet." The men rose from their seats and moved out to the Promenade Deck to see what had happened. A young man from Sweden, Bjornstrom Steffanson, later reported that he heard one of the men cry out that the ship had hit an iceberg.

Men working in the boiler rooms near the collision heard the loudest noises, which they described as crunching sounds similar to thunder. Stewardess Violet Jessop and her cabin mate heard a crunching sound, then felt the ship stop.

Down in the stokers' area, the men heard plenty of noise and saw, and felt, the water pouring in. One of the firemen later said: "My section was about one-third of the ship's length from the bows, and we found that the whole of the starboard side was smashed in as far as our section. Well, we got into the next section aft and there we stayed, for, being on watch, it was our business to stay. I did not think, and nobody thought at the time, that the *Titanic* could sink."

The calm seas and fair weather that the Titanic *traveled through made spotting icebergs like this one very difficult. Rough water splashing against the icebergs would have made them easier to detect.*

strewn on the decks, but no one appeared nervous, and no one panicked. There were no signs that anything serious had happened to the great ship. Some Third Class passengers even played with the ice, throwing chunks of it around as if taking part in a snowball fight. Some slid, laughing, across the icy deck. The ship continued to stand tall in the water, seemingly invincible.

Deeper in the ship, however, people knew better. Some of the stokers in the boiler rooms had heard a loud booming noise and been sprayed with cold water. They fled from their workroom, knowing something to be wrong.

Captain Smith hurried to ask First Officer Murdoch what the ship had hit. Together they went to inspect the damage while Smith sent Fourth Officer Joseph Boxhall to check another area of the ship. There were no signs of water on any of the decks, so Smith told Boxhall to find the ship's carpenter and have him conduct an inspection. When he was finished, the carpenter solemnly told the officers on the bridge, "The ship is making water."[37] Boxhall found that two boiler rooms had been flooded and that the mail room, on F Deck, was soaked.

The ship's chief designer, Thomas Andrews, was summoned and he, too, rushed down to the hold. There water was surging into the compartments faster than the men operating the pumps could remove it. Andrews realized that nothing could be done to prevent the first five compartments from flooding. The *Titanic* was doomed.

5 To the Boats!

The ship's designer, Thomas Andrews, gave Captain Edward Smith the devastating news: the *Titanic* had only an hour, or at best an hour and a half, before it sank. Hearing this, the captain must have been painfully aware that tragedy loomed. The ship had only sixteen standard wooden lifeboats and four collapsible ones on board, enough to save less than half the passengers and crew. As captain, he knew that he himself was obliged to go down with his ship if the worst happened.

Harold Cottam, the wireless operator for the Carpathia, *a steamer on its way to the Mediterranean, was the first to receive* Titanic's *distress calls.*

Captain Smith had already spoken with White Star managing director Bruce Ismay, who came to the bridge wearing his pajamas. Ismay asked the captain what had happened and was informed about the collision. "Do you think the ship is seriously damaged?" asked Ismay. "I am afraid she is,"[38] Smith replied.

Meanwhile, the crew worked frantically to prevent more water from entering the ship. Every man who could be spared was ordered to the pumps. The engineering department struggled to keep the electricity operating. Power and lights were critical for the tasks that had to be done on that harrowing night.

Save Our Ship!

Up in the wireless room, radio operators Bride and Phillips knew that the *Titanic* was in bad shape. Captain Smith had ordered them to send out distress calls reporting the accident and describing their location in the North Atlantic, which Fourth Officer Boxhall had calculated.

The first distress call from the *Titanic* was recorded on the *Carpathia*, the closest ship, at 12:15 A.M. on April 15. It read: "Have struck an iceberg. We are badly

Just Out of Reach

Less than twenty miles from the endangered decks of the *Titanic*, another ship stood in the Atlantic—close enough to come to their aid, it seemed. The crew on that ship, the *Californian*, had also noticed another ship in the distance and wondered about it.

Captain Stanley Lord of the *Californian* later said that the ship he saw did not look like a passenger liner but rather like a medium-sized steamer. Later, officers and other crew members aboard the *Californian* said that they saw eight rockets fired from a ship the night of April 14–15 and so informed their captain. He suggested that they signal the other ship, using a Morse lamp. When they received no response, they wrongly concluded that the rockets were set off for some other purpose, perhaps a festive event. Some crew members said they thought they saw the other ship steam away, heading southwest.

Ernest Gill, a crew member on the *Californian*, later gave sworn testimony that he and some other crew members thought the rockets they'd seen were a sign of distress that their captain should heed. Gill also swore that he heard the second engineer of the *Californian* say, "Why the devil didn't they wake up the [*Californian*'s] wireless man?" Gill knew he would lose his job after he gave his statement, but he commented anyway that "no captain who refuses or neglects to give aid to a vessel in distress should be able to hush up the men."

damaged. Lat. 41.46 N., long. 50.14 W."[39] In calling for help the operators used the code letters CQD, which means "Come Quick, Danger," and MGY, the code symbol for the *Titanic*. They tapped out these letters in the series of dots and dashes used by Morse code.

The *Titanic*'s radio operators were also among the first, if not the very first, to use the SOS distress signal. Bride later said that he urged Phillips to try the new call, which had been chosen for its simplicity (three dots, three dashes, three dots). The two men were joking as they sent out the calls, to keep up their spirits. In that same vein, Bride told Phillips, "This may be your last chance to send it."[40]

Harold Cottam, the wireless operator for the *Carpathia*, received the first message by sheer accident. He was technically off duty but had kept his headset on while getting ready for bed. Cottam was shocked. He sent back this message: "Shall I tell my captain? Do you require assistance?"[41] The *Titanic* answered, "Yes."[42]

Captain Smith authorized the *Titanic*'s crew to send up distress rockets to signal any ships close enough to help. The lights of one ship looked especially close and were not moving. Between 12:45 and 1:45, the crew of the *Titanic* lit eight white rockets, the universal signal of distress, and sent them into the sky. The rockets, fired at five-minute intervals, exploded noisily. They had glowing tails and left a shower of white stars. Officer Boxhall was convinced that the ship in the distance was close enough to read a Morse signal. He therefore requested and received permission from Captain Smith to use a signaling lamp to send the message "Come at once, we are sinking."[43]

Of the ships that responded to the distress calls, only one was close enough to act in this emergency. The *Carpathia* was fifty-eight miles away, bound east for the Mediterranean. Its captain, Arthur H. Rostron, immediately changed course and steamed northeast toward the *Titanic* at a speed of some fourteen to sixteen knots. However, the *Carpathia* was older and slower than the *Titanic* and would have to skirt ice along the way. It could take four to five hours for it to reach the stricken ship.

Meanwhile, the *Titanic* was steadily dying. As each compartment filled with water, it overflowed the bulkheads (compartment walls) and the next section began to flood. After the first five compartments filled, the ship began to dip down at the bow (the front).

"Get the Lifeboats Ready"

Soon after midnight, Captain Smith ordered the crew to uncover the lifeboats. At 12:30, the captain ordered all the passengers on deck so that the lifeboats could be loaded and then lowered over the sides of the sinking ship.

The ship's barber, August H. Weikman, later said that after the collision he saw Thomas Andrews instructing the crew to get the steerage passengers up on deck. Mr. Dodd, the second steward, said, "All hands to man the lifeboats, also to put on lifebelts."[44]

The Carpathia *was fifty-eight miles away from the* Titanic *when it responded to its distress signal. It would take four hours to reach the first of* Titanic's *lifeboats.*

Other members of the crew were told, "All hands on deck! Bring your lifebelts [lifejackets]!"[45] The stewards and stewardesses were told to prepare the passengers. Thomas Andrews told one stewardess, "Tell them to put on warm clothing, see that everyone has a life belt and get them all up to the Boat Deck."[46] Andrews himself never donned a lifejacket. He was to spend the next fateful hours alerting people and helping load and lower the lifeboats.

In the period immediately after the collision, the crew went about their duties, outwardly calm, and the passengers did not show signs of panic. Groups of people wearing life preservers could be seen on the deck, where they stood shivering in the cold air.

Some passengers received no direct information about the crash or instructions to put on their lifejackets. Others received confusing or conflicting information. First Class passenger Emily (Mrs. William) Ryerson later described her experiences:

> I rang and asked the steward, Bishop, what was the matter. He said, "There is talk of an iceberg, ma'am, and they have stopped, not to run into it." I told him to keep me informed if there were any orders. It was bitterly cold so I put on a warm wrapper and looked out the window and saw the stars shining and a calm sea but I heard no noise. . . . After about 10 minutes I went out in the corridor and saw far off people hurrying on deck. A passenger ran by and called out, "Put on your lifebelts and come up to the boat deck." I said, "Where did you get those orders?" He said, "From the captain."[47]

Ryerson then awakened her husband, children, and maid. They all dressed and put on their lifebelts, then walked to the

Even with life preservers, the chances of surviving in the 28 degree waters of the Atlantic were not very good. Many who did not get into a lifeboat froze to death in the frigid waters.

Boat Deck, where they waited for further information.

Stewardess Violet Jessop dressed and was prepared to return on duty after the collision. Then a white-faced steward knocked on her door and said, "You know the ship is sinking?"[48] As she later wrote,

> Sinking? Of course *Titanic* couldn't be sinking! What nonsense! She so perfect, so new—yet now she was so still, so inanimate, not a sound after that awful grinding crash. . . . My mind could not accept the fact that this superperfect creation was to do so futile a thing as sink.[49]

Jessop had not brought a warm coat or hat along on the trip, so she borrowed a scarf to tie around her head. As she passed an open cabin, she popped in to grab a quilt to warm herself. She later recalled, "How strange it was to pass all those rooms lit up so brilliantly, their doors open and contents lying around in disorder. Jewels sparkled on dressing tables and a pair of silver slippers were lying just where they had been kicked off."[50]

Courage Under Pressure

According to eyewitnesses, some passengers remained stoic as the end approached and even gave up chances to be saved. One of the ship's barbers urged Colonel John Jacob Astor to don a lifejacket and jump from the sinking ship. But he said, "I am not going to jump," and remained standing as the ship made its final plunge into the icy waters.

Another American millionaire, Benjamin Guggenheim, and his valet Victor Giglio were seen on the deck dressed in their best evening clothes and without lifejackets. Guggenheim reportedly told a steward, "We've dressed in our best and are prepared to go down like gentlemen." If the steward survived, requested Guggenheim, he should tell Mrs. Guggenheim that her dead husband had done his duty.

When Mahala Douglas urged her husband, Walter, to join her in her lifeboat, he refused, saying, "No; I must be a gentleman." Douglas did not survive.

The poignant story of Isidor and Ida Straus was widely reported. Mr. Straus, old and rather feeble, was urged to take a seat in a lifeboat, but he refused special treatment. His wife, who had started to enter a boat, then got out, saying, "We have been living together many years and where you go I go." Then, before the Straus's maid climbed into the lifeboat, Mrs. Straus removed her own fur coat and wrapped it around the young woman, saying, "It will be cold in the lifeboat, and I do not need it any more." Archibald Gracie said that the couple then sat down together on deck chairs to await their fate.

In the mail room, three American and two British mail clerks had struggled in vain to save thousands of bags of mail, including two hundred sacks of registered mail and hundreds of parcels. The five men worked against the rising water to carry the heavy sacks to higher ground. All these men perished. An article in the Brooklyn *Daily Eagle* said, "Not one can say that they attempted to get into the lifeboats or thought of themselves for a single instant."

Not one of the engineers, electricians, plumbers, or boiler-room crew survived the sinking of the *Titanic* either. All remained loyally at their posts, laboring amid dreadful conditions to provide the vessel with power and light until the end.

Desperate Effort

The lifeboats on the *Titanic* were stored on the top, or boat, deck, covered with tarpaulins in mechanisms called davits. To operate them, the crew had to unfasten the boats from their metal support poles, then use ropes and pulleys to lower them over the side down to the next deck, where the passengers could step inside. The crew had never used these lifeboats or this particular equipment before. Neither passengers nor crew were well prepared for catastrophe. No lifeboat drills had been held on the *Titanic*, and the passengers had not been assigned to specific lifeboats.

With the aid of male volunteers, crewmen helped people into the boats. It was necessary to step in carefully lest one topple the boat while it was suspended in midair. According to the etiquette and common practice of that era, the women and children were saved first. To the men he saw standing on the boat deck, Thomas Andrews was heard to say, "Now, men, remember you are Englishmen. Women and children first."[51]

However, many passengers, both male and female, simply refused to go into the first boats. To some the ship seemed much safer than a tiny wooden boat dangling high above a vast expanse of dark, cold water. Perhaps they also thought rescue was

The women and children were loaded into the lifeboats first. Many of the men parted with their wives and children and remained on the deck to conserve space in the boats.

In order to keep spirits up, the band on the Titanic *continued to play on the deck as the lifeboats were lowered into the water. Not one member of the band survived.*

imminent—the lights of what appeared to be a ship could be seen on the horizon.

The first lifeboat to be loaded and lowered was number seven. Officer Murdoch, in charge on that side of the ship, oversaw the loading. When he could not fill the boat with women and children, Murdoch permitted men to join their wives or friends in the boat. But he could still find only twenty-eight persons who wished to board.

An eight-year-old boy, Marshall Drew, was in boat eleven with his aunt. Drew later said, "Elevators were not running. We walked up to the boat deck. All was calm and orderly. An officer was in charge. 'Women and children first' [he said], as he directed lifeboat number 11 to be filled. There were many tearful farewells. We and Uncle Jim said 'Good bye.'"[52]

Mrs. Leah Aks, a Third Class passenger, was distraught when she was separated from her infant son Frank after he was tossed into boat eleven, which was nearly full. Elizabeth Nye took the baby and wrapped him in a steamer blanket while Mrs. Aks was guided to boat thirteen. Another passenger, Mrs. Selena Cook, tried to console her. (Cook later helped Aks reclaim her infant son.)

Among the other women who boarded lifeboats were Mrs. J. J. (Margaret, or Molly) Brown and Madeleine Astor. An eyewitness later reported that Jack Astor had asked Officer Lightoller for permission to accompany his wife in the lifeboat, since she was pregnant. But Lightoller declined, explaining, "No men are allowed on these boats until the women are loaded first."[53] Accordingly, Astor insisted that his wife get into the boat and promised her he would soon follow.

As the passengers entered the lifeboats, the eight musicians on board continued playing to boost their spirits. These were the quintet, led by violinist Wallace Hartley, and the trio, which played the violin, cello, and piano in the reception room. They had come together to do their part during the emergency and had begun playing shortly after midnight in the First Class lounge. Survivors would later recall that the groups played ragtime tunes, waltzes, and other lighthearted music. After the water on the promenade deck rose too high, the musicians moved up to the boat deck.

As the boats were being loaded, the ship's bellboys, most of them only fourteen or fifteen years old, brought loaves of bread up to the boat deck. The bread, which had been baked for the next day's meals, was placed in the lifeboats. Stewards and stew-

Not Enough Boats

In his original plans for the *Titanic*, designer Thomas Andrews had provided for sixty-eight lifeboats, which would have held 3,538 people. But the owners decided these boats would take up too much space and detract from the ship's appearance. Besides, the law did not require them to carry nearly as many lifeboats.

In order to meet British Board of Trade regulations, the *Titanic* needed to stock lifeboats for only 962 persons. The lifeboats on the ship could actually accommodate 1,178 persons, which exceeded the requirements but was still not nearly enough for the 3,547 on board when the ship was full. The laws that prescribed the number of lifeboats required on a passenger liner had last been updated in 1894, at a time when ships were much smaller and carried far fewer people.

These rules had been strongly influenced by the steamship companies' owners, who preferred not to devote a great deal of deck space to lifeboats. To do so would mean giving up space devoted to sports facilities, lounges, and other amenities, and would also make the deck look less inviting.

Policy makers contended that large, modern ships did not really need lifeboats for everyone on board anyway. It was true that heavy steamships did not sink during storms or in turbulent waters, as older-style vessels sometimes did. And with radios on board, ships could call for help. If a disaster occurred, lifeboats would be needed only to convey groups of people from the sinking ship to the rescue ship.

Would more people have been saved if there had been more lifeboats on the *Titanic*? Sir Alfred Chalmers, an advisor to the British Board of Trade, later told investigators that the crew of the *Titanic* lacked the time to launch more boats even if they'd had them. Chalmers argued that "in abnormally fine weather with a still sea and with two clear hours it was only possible to deal with eighteen boats . . . two boats being on deck when the ship sank."

ardesses added extra blankets and lifejackets they found in empty staterooms.

As the crew rushed to lower the boats, boat fifteen almost struck number thirteen.

Before the lowering tackle could be cut from thirteen, which reached the water first, its occupants saw number fifteen coming down on top of them. A crewman managed to cut the tackle in time for the passengers to push their boat out of danger. Then as lifeboats became scarcer and the ship dipped farther forward, more people wanted to get into the remaining boats.

The Titanic *had only sixteen standard, wooden lifeboats and four collapsible ones. It was later argued that even if there were more boats available, the crew would not have had the time to load them.*

A DECK
70 feet above
the water

"B" DECK
from which many
of the women were
taken into the boats

While Murdoch was supervising loading the boats on one side of the boat deck, Second Officer Charles Lightoller oversaw the loading of those on the other side. He later said that

> between one boat being lowered away and the next being prepared I usually nipped along to have a look down the very long emergency staircase leading direct from the Boat Deck down to C Deck . . . [which] served my purpose now to gauge the speed with which the water was rising, and how high it had got. . . . That cold green water, crawling its ghostly way up that staircase, was a sight that stamped itself in my memory. Step by step, it made its way up.[54]

"The Agony of It"

It was about 1:10 A.M. when the first lifeboat pulled away from the *Titanic*. The calm surface of the sea allowed the boats to land relatively easily. Even so, Violet Jessop said that her boat hit the water with "a terrific thud, a bone-cracking thud."[55]

As the water rose up the deck and reached the bridge, Archibald Gracie and some crew members who had been loading the lifeboats walked toward the stern. As he recalled,

> we had taken but a few steps . . . when there arose before us from the decks below, a mass of humanity several lines deep, covering the Boat Deck, facing us, and completely blocking our passage toward the stern. There were women in the crowd, as well as men, and they seemed to be steerage passengers who had just come up from the

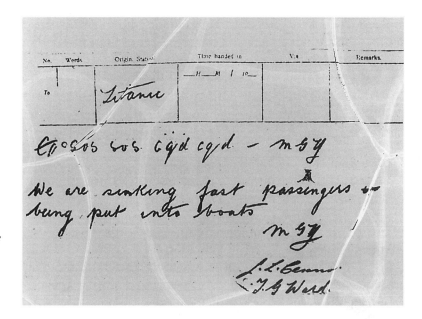

This is the last radio message sent by the Titanic *before she went down with over sixteen hundred passengers still onboard.*

decks below. Instantly, when they saw us and the water on the deck chasing us from behind, they turned in the opposite direction toward the stern. . . . Even among these people there was no agonized cry, or evidence of panic, but oh, the agony of it![56]

The American male millionaires—Astor, Widener, Thayer, and some others—stood on the boat deck, watching. Another group, made up of Archibald Butt, Clarence Moore, Francis Millet, and William Ryerson, went on playing cards in the smoking room almost as if nothing unusual were happening.

"The Last Boat Left"

By 1:30 A.M. the passengers could feel, and see, the decks sloping downward and the bow of the ship inclining toward the water. As the ship slanted forward, the stern slowly rose. As this was happening, the power on the *Titanic* was fading.

Lively music still filled the air, however, at 2:05 as the last boat was being launched. None of the boats was filled to capacity, and some were only half full. The crew would later say they had been worried that the boats might tip over if they were fully loaded with people. However, Harland & Wolff had tested them beforehand and found that they could move safely up and down with a full load.

Several crew members were desperately trying to release one more boat, a collapsible one stored near a smokestack. As Harold Bride, the assistant wireless operator, later recalled, "I saw a collapsible boat near a funnel, and went over to it. Twelve men were trying to boost it down to the Boat Deck. They were having an awful time. It was the last boat left. I looked at it longingly a few minutes; then I gave a hand and over she went."[57]

Archibald Gracie was one of the male passengers who helped women and children board the lifeboats. He later described the scene.

> I was now working with the crew at the davits [movable cranes] on the starboard side forward, adjusting them, ready for lowering the Engelhardt boat from the roof of the officers' house to the Boat Deck below. Some one of the crew on the roof, where it was, sang out, "Has any passenger a knife?"[58]

Gracie offered his small penknife, "if that will do any good."[59] Later he said, "It appeared to me then that there was more trouble than there ought to have been in removing the canvas cover and cutting the boat loose, and that some means should have been available for doing this without delay."[60]

As the ship slumped forward, the more than fifteen hundred people who had not boarded lifeboats moved away from the sinking bow of the ship toward the stern. Two priests on board prayed with them and heard the last confessions of those who were Catholics. The Catholic passengers recited their rosaries.

Those who remained inside saw the water rise up the steps of the Grand Staircase. After the last boat—actually more of a raft—had left, Harold Bride returned to the radio room to tell Phillips, who was still diligently working the wireless. Captain Smith had been making the rounds of the ship to release his crew from their duties. He instructed Bride and Phillips: "Men, you have done your full duty. You can do no more. Abandon your cabin. Now it's every man for himself."[61]

6 Terrifying Hours

As the *Titanic* plunged deeper and deeper into the water, a giant wave swept across her sagging decks. More than a thousand people tried desperately to hang on to parts of the ship as salt water poured over them. Some victims were washed out to sea; others maintained their footing. Some decided it was time to jump.

Chief John Collins and a deck steward were helping a steerage passenger and her two children when the wave struck. Collins was swept overboard while holding the woman's baby in his arms. The baby was wrenched away. The other three people also disappeared.

August Weikman, the ship's barber, was washed overboard too. As he swam toward an object he spotted in the dark water, he heard an explosion that may have been when a boiler blew up. Climbing onto some floating deck chairs, he saw the bodies of people who had been killed or injured by the explosion.

Seventeen-year-old Jack Thayer jumped into the sea as the ship went down. As he later recalled, "I was pushed out and then sucked down."[62] Breathlessly, he plummeted in the frigid water. But Thayer, a strong swimmer, managed to move away from the *Titanic*. He surfaced about forty yards from the ship as it was going down.

By about 2:17 A.M. the ship was standing on end, stern up, dropping faster and faster into the water. Her lights blinked once, then took on a red hue as they faded away. Officer Lightoller recalled it clearly:

> All the lights suddenly went out, and with a roar, every one of the gigantic boilers left their beds and went crashing down through bulkheads and everything that stood in their way. Crowds of people were still on the after deck and at the stern, but the end was near.[63]

As one of the immense funnels fell, smoking and sparking, it nearly hit Jack Thayer. Once again, he was drawn into the freezing water. This time, however, he resurfaced beside the overturned collapsible boat, and some of the men helped him on to it.

This was Collapsible Boat B, which Officer Lightoller had helped release at the last moment, using Archibald Gracie's pocket knife. Lightoller himself had gone down with the ship. But then a rush of hot air had pushed him away from it and he emerged amid floating bodies. Pulled under once more, Lightoller swam back up and reached the boat Thayer had boarded. Wireless operator Harold Bride also went down, then managed to swim to the upturned collapsible. The small group of survivors lay shivering on this unsteady craft.

As the front compartments filled with water, the Titanic's stern rose into the air. Some survivors say they saw the ship break in two before she completely went under at just before 2:30 A.M. on April 15, 1912.

"Motionless"

Just before its final plunge at 2:20 A.M., the *Titanic* seemed to lie flat for a moment, with its stern straight up. Survivors later told different stories about what happened next. Some people claimed the ship seemed to break before sinking; others said it sank in one piece. Jack Thayer recalled it like this:

> We could see groups of the almost fifteen hundred people still aboard, clinging in clusters or bunches, like swarming bees; only to fall in masses, pairs or singly, as the great after part of the ship, two hundred and fifty feet of it, rose into the sky, till it reached a sixty-five or seventy-degree angle. Here it seemed to pause, and just hung, for what felt like minutes. Gradually she turned her deck away from us, as though to hide from our sight the awful spectacle.[64]

Lawrence Beesley's lifeboat was one or two miles away when the ship went down. He said that

> all in the lifeboat were motionless as we watched the ship in absolute silence—save some who would not look and buried their heads on each others' shoulders. . . . As we gazed awestruck, she tilted slightly up, revolving apparently about a center of gravity just astern of amidships until she attained a vertical upright position, and there she remained—motionless! As she swung up, her lights, which had shown without a flicker all night, went out suddenly, then came on again for a single flash and then went out altogether.[65]

Martha Stevenson was among those who could not bear to watch the ship sink. She later said, "When the call came that she was going I covered my face and then heard someone call, 'She's broken.'"[66] In Collapsible Boat C, Bruce Ismay also looked away.

Mahala Douglas said, "I heard no explosion. I watched the boat go down, and the last picture to my mind is the immense mass of black against the star-lit sky, and then—nothingness."[67]

Another survivor, Archibald Gracie, was underwater when the ship sank. The athletic Gracie had jumped into a rising wave, holding his breath. Once he surfaced, he grabbed some pieces of wood to keep himself afloat, then looked around:

> I could see no *Titanic* in sight. She had entirely disappeared beneath the calm surface of the ocean and without a sign of any wave. That the sea had swallowed her up with all her precious belongings was indicated by the slight sound of a gulp behind me as the water closed over her.[68]

"Cries of Death"

The ship gone, hundreds of people were left struggling in the water. Numerous corpses floated to the surface. Bits and pieces of wreckage bobbed around them.

For those stranded in the sea, there was little hope of surviving, even with life-jackets. The temperature was 28 degrees Fahrenheit—below freezing—and most of the lifeboats had rowed away. Some of the seamen in charge of the boats feared they

---

"A Terrible Noise"

Survivors later described what they saw and heard as the *Titanic* disappeared. A thin veil of smoke seemed to hang over the water where the ship went down. Lawrence Beesley described the incredible noise he heard at that time:

> It has always seemed to me that it was nothing but the engines and machinery coming loose from their place and bearings and falling through the compartments, smashing everything in their way. It was partly a roar, partly a groan, partly a rattle and partly a smash, and it was not a sudden roar as an explosion would be; it went on successively for some seconds, possibly fifteen or twenty, as the heavy machinery dropped down to the bottom (now the bows) of the ship. . . . But it was a noise no one had heard before and no one wishes to hear again. It was stupefying, stupendous, as it came to us along the water. It was as if all the heavy things one could think of had been thrown downstairs from the top of a house, smashing each other and the stairs and everything in the way.

Archibald Gracie, who was a very strong swimmer, was one of the few to survive the freezing waters that the Titanic *went down in. Of all those who plunged into the icy Atlantic, only twelve survived.*

would be engulfed by the suction that would be created when the *Titanic* sank. Several lifeboats were moving toward the unknown ship whose lights gleamed in the distance. The occupants hoped to ask for assistance there and have them return to the *Titanic* for other passengers.

Frantic cries came from the water. Archibald Gracie called them "agonizing cries of death from over a thousand throats, the wails and groans of the suffering, the shrieks of the terror-stricken and the awful gaspings for breath of those in the last throes of drowning."[69]

Gracie managed to reach Collapsible Boat B. Fifteen men were already clinging to it when he pulled himself on board. He later recalled that "no extending hand was held out to me."[70] Eventually, about thirty men clung to this upturned boat, carefully positioned so they would not capsize it.

Only twelve of the hundreds of people who remained floating in their lifejackets survived. They were picked up by boats that returned after the ship went down. However, few boats did come back. In Boat Eight, Seaman Thomas Jones suggested that they return for more, but the three men rowing that boat refused, claiming that their boat would be overturned as people scrambled to climb in. Gladys Cherry, an English passenger who agreed with Seaman Jones, later claimed that he told them, "Ladies, if any of us are saved, remember I wanted to go back. I would rather drown with them than leave them."[71] Molly Brown met the same resistance when she urged her fellow survivors in Boat Six to row back to the scene.

Boats Eleven and Fifteen could do little to help. They contained about seventy passengers each and could hardly move. The people in Boat Nine, also crowded, feared they would sink if they tried to return. Boat Thirteen was full, and there were no seamen aboard to row toward those who needed help. The occupants included stewards, a fireman, cooks, and some passengers. Ruth Becker later described the situation.

> Lifeboat number 13 that I was in had about 65 people in it so it was filled to standing room with men and women in every conceivable condition of dress and undress. It was bitter cold—a curious, deadening, bitter cold. And then with all of this, there fell on the ear the most terrible noises that human beings ever listened to—the cries of hundreds of people struggling in the icy cold water, crying for help with a cry that we knew could not be answered. We wanted to pick up some of

those swimming, but this would have meant swamping our boat and further loss of the lives of all of us.[72]

The cries of the people in the water gradually faded, then stopped. However, years later, the survivors were haunted by memories of these moments. Jack Thayer sadly observed after the event that

> the partially filled lifeboats standing by, only a few hundred yards away, never came back. Why on earth they did not come back is a mystery. How could any human being fail to heed those cries? The most heart-rending part of the whole tragedy was the failure, right after the *Titanic* sank, of those boats which were only partially loaded, to pick up the poor souls in the water.[73]

From Boat Fourteen, Fifth Officer Harold Lowe worked to save lives. He distributed his passengers throughout boats that had room, then grouped Boats Four, Ten, Twelve, and Collapsible Boat D together. Raising the sail on his boat, he took several men back to search for survivors. They found only four people still alive among numerous dead bodies and pieces of wreckage but continued to search until sunrise.

Tense Hours

The *Titanic*'s survivors faced many dangers as they floated on the icy North Atlantic in small wooden boats waiting for rescue. Few boats held experienced seamen, and they all lacked basic equipment, such as lights.

Mrs. J. Stuart White found herself in a lifeboat with twenty-two women and four men. Two of the men had told the officer who was loading the boat that they could row. But Mrs. White later complained that

> the men in our boat were anything but seamen, with the exception of one man. The women all rowed, every one of them. Miss Young rowed every minute. The men could not row, they did not know the first thing about it. Mrs. Swift, from Brooklyn, rowed every minute also, except when she was throwing up, which she did six or seven times. Countess Rothes stood at the

Fifth Officer Harold Lowe took some empty lifeboats back to the site where Titanic *sank. He searched until sunrise and found only four survivors.*

tiller. Where would we have been if it had not been for our women, with such men as that put in charge of the boat?[74]

Many Third Class passengers, including emigrants who spoke no English, were in Boat Sixteen. They prayed a great deal while their boat tossed about in the ice-strewn sea for nearly three hours.

The people on the two collapsible boats faced special threats. Waves splashed over their heads as they also prayed during these harrowing hours. Finding themselves to be a mixture of Catholics and Protestants, the group recited "The Lord's Prayer" over and over while scanning the horizon for a rescue ship. They had to work hard to keep their overturned boat in balance. Archibald Gracie later wrote of the experience.

We all suffered from cold and exposure. The boat was so loaded down with the heavy weight it carried that it became partly submerged, and the water washed up to our waists as we lay in our reclining position. Several of our companions near the stern of the boat, unable to stand the exposure and strain, gave up the struggle and fell off.[75]

"Take Us Off!"

At about 3:30 A.M. the survivors spied a ship's lights in the distance and saw signal rockets on its decks. The lights grew closer. The survivors who were still able to row headed toward the lights. The sea had

Survivors of the Titanic *row toward the* Carpathia *on the morning of April 15, 1912. Of the more than two thousand passengers onboard, only 866 were rescued.*

The "Unsinkable" Molly Brown

Molly Brown.

One of the most colorful people aboard the *Titanic* was Margaret (Molly) Brown. She was the Missouri-born wife of James Joseph (J. J.) Brown, a Colorado miner who came into $2 million in 1884 when a mine under his supervision hit a rich vein of gold.

Molly Brown became known for her warm, down-to-earth manner as well as her flashy clothing and jewels. However, she was snubbed by the wealthy social matrons of Denver, who looked down on the newly rich couple. Brown then moved to Newport, Rhode Island, where she found that people were much wealthier than those in Denver. These easterners, who had been rich for generations, regarded Molly as an amusing and interesting companion. Brown also made friends with prominent Europeans, who enjoyed her unpretentious manner and humorous stories about life in the mining country.

By 1912 Brown felt at home on luxury liners like the *Titanic*. As the ship was sinking, Brown kept urging her friends to board lifeboats when two male friends picked her up and put her into Boat Six as it was being lowered. In it, Brown helped with the oars, encouraging her fellow passengers as they rowed and awaited rescue. She wrapped her sable stole around a shivering stoker. Nobody on her lifeboat died that night.

When reporters in New York City interviewed Molly Brown after the disaster, she declared, "I'm unsinkable!" People thus began calling her "the Unsinkable Mrs. Brown," and she was cheered as a heroine wherever she went, including Denver, which she visited briefly after the *Titanic* disaster.

Many stories, often spurious, sprang up about the vivacious Molly and her husband. J. J. Brown was a mine superintendent, not a wild and crazy prospector as some said. The real-life Molly Brown was an intelligent woman who spoke several languages, not the unschooled bumpkin sometimes portrayed in legend.

A Spirited Commander

Captain Arthur H. Rostron commanded the Cunard liner *Carpathia*, which rescued the *Titanic* survivors. The forty-two-year-old Rostron had first gone to sea at the age of thirteen and was known for his energy, quick thinking, and strong religious beliefs.

At 12:55 A.M. on April 15, the *Carpathia's* wireless operator, Harold Cottam, had rushed into Rostron's office to announce that the *Titanic* was in distress. Rostron was then moving south toward the Mediterranean, but he ordered the crew to change direction immediately and estimated they would reach the disaster site in four hours.

Rostron issued a stream of orders to prepare for the rescue. He assigned three doctors on board to receive patients in each of the three dining rooms, where they would work with assistants. Crew members were told to direct incoming survivors to the proper place. The crew was to carry supplies and medical equipment to various rooms and prepare tea, coffee, and soup for the surviving passengers and crew members. The survivors' names were to be recorded and sent out by wireless. His cabin, all officers' cabins, the smoking rooms, the library, and the dining rooms would be used to house survivors. Rostron later said, "To all I strictly enjoined the necessity for order, discipline, and quietness and to avoid all confusion."

Above all, Rostron had to avoid the treacherous ice floes throughout the area while moving at full speed. He posted extra lookouts with superior eyesight throughout the ship. They spotted six icebergs. Interestingly, these bergs were first seen from the bridge, not the crow's nest in the bow where the regular lookouts were.

The *Carpathia* arrived on the site in three and a half hours. At the scene, Rostron saw the iceberg that had destroyed the *Titanic*. The part of the iceberg that stood above sea level was only about one-ninth the size of its entire mass. (This peculiarity gave rise to the popular saying "that's just the tip of the iceberg," meaning a situation that contains hidden dangers or problems under the surface.)

Captain Rostron later told a friend that "when day broke, and I saw the ice I had steamed through during the night, I shuddered, and could only think that some other Hand than mine was on that helm during the night."

been calm all night, but now it was becoming increasingly choppy. Ruth Becker recalled that "our tiny boat bounced around like a cork."[76]

As the *Carpathia* arrived upon the scene, its crew was stunned to see a huge field of ice to the west. Large individual icebergs protruded from this long mass. Many other icebergs lay behind their ship.

The *Titanic*'s lifeboats were scattered around an area about four miles in diameter. Fourth Officer Boxhall had placed green flares in his boat, Number Two, to alert possible rescuers and guide other lifeboats toward him. Seeing those flares, the rescue ship approached Boat Two first. At 4:10 A.M. its occupants boarded the *Carpathia*.

Having finished his search for survivors, Officer Lowe now worked to get people safely aboard the *Carpathia*. Spotting Collapsible Boat D lying low in the water, he decided to tow them to the rescue ship. Collapsible Boat A was also in bad shape, with more than a foot of water inside, and it could not move. Boat A had originally held about thirty people, but now only one woman and a dozen men remained. Lowe sailed over and took them on board. A woman who survived aboard Boat Fourteen later said that "Mr. Lowe's manly bearing gave us all confidence. As I look back now he seems to me to personify the best traditions of the British sailor."[77]

The men clinging to Collapsible Boat B feared that nobody could see them. But Officer Lightoller found his whistle in his pocket, and the crew members on Boats Twelve and Four responded to it. As they drew near, Lightoller cried, "Come over and take us off!"[78] The boats had to move cautiously toward the overturned raft so the men could climb in. After the others

The Carpathia*'s captain, Arthur Henry Rostron, was awarded the Congressional Medal of Honor for his bravery in rescuing the survivors of the ill-fated* Titanic.

were safe, Lightoller joined them and the boat headed for the *Carpathia*. It was then about 6:30 A.M.

As each lifeboat stopped alongside the rescue ship, its cold, frightened people were taken aboard. Those who had enough energy climbed up rope ladders; the others were pulled up in nets or slings. Those suffering from exposure, shock, or both were given warm blankets and coats and helped to resting places on chairs or the deck. Fortunately, the *Carpathia* was only half full, so all the *Titanic*'s survivors could stay together.

The *Carpathia*'s regular passengers were stunned to wake up amid ice-strewn waters. Looking out her porthole, Mrs. Wallace Bradford wondered why she saw a "rocky" shore when the ship was in mid-ocean, presumably going south toward the Mediterranean.[79] Passengers were urged to remain in their cabins. When one noticed disheveled women entering the dining room, a stewardess sadly told him, "From the *Titanic*. She's at the bottom of the ocean."[80]

First Class passengers on the *Carpathia* offered their cabins to the survivors who seemed most in need. Others stayed in the public rooms, which were made into dormitories. Its captain, Arthur Rostron, gave his own rooms to Mrs. Astor, Mrs. Widener, and Mrs. Thayer.

The Final Count

As the survivors were brought on board, they looked for loved ones, friends, and crew members. An Italian mother was reunited with her two children. Jack Thayer found his mother. The Carter family was reunited. Harold Bride realized that his coworker, Jack Phillips, had died in a collapsible boat from exposure. Women who had been hoping to see their husbands now realized they had perished. Young people had lost fathers, and sometimes mothers. A final count showed 705 survivors. All the others, 1,503 people, were dead.

One survivor, J. Bruce Ismay, appeared to be in shock. When he heard that many women had died, Ismay said he should have gone down with the ship himself. He refused all food except soup. The *Carpathia*'s worried physician placed him in his own small room and asked Jack Thayer to visit Ismay. As Thayer later said,

[Ismay] was seated, in his pyjamas, on his bunk, staring straight ahead, shaking all over like a leaf. . . . I am almost certain that on the *Titanic* his hair had been black with slight tinges of gray, but now his hair was virtually snow white. I have never seen a man so completely wrecked. Nothing I could do or say brought any response.[81]

For four hours, the *Carpathia* combed the waters at the site. They found only pieces of wreckage and dead bodies amid the ice.

Captain Rostron announced that the *Carpathia* would pause above the spot where it was probable that the *Titanic* had sunk. There an Episcopal priest on board led the group in a brief memorial service for those who had died and gave a prayer of thanks for those still alive.

Sad Journey

With its flag flying at half-mast, the *Carpathia* prepared to leave the site, knowing that another ship, the *Californian*, was on its way. It was a 6,223-ton cargo ship traveling from Liverpool, England, to Boston. At 5:30 A.M., the *Californian*'s wireless operator returned to duty and heard about the fate of the *Titanic* from another ship, the *Virginian*. He ran to tell his captain, "The *Titanic* has hit a berg and sunk!"[82]

Communicating by wireless, the *Californian* told the *Carpathia* that it would continue to hunt for survivors after the *Carpathia* left with its passengers to New York. However, they found only abandoned lifeboats and floating debris—deck chairs, pieces of wood, cushions. After several futile hours, the *Californian* also headed for America.

As the *Carpathia* steamed west, its radio operator, Harold Cottam, was flooded with work. Harold Bride was exhausted and suffering from frostbitten feet, but he insisted on helping Cottam. Together they tapped out a list of the survivors. The men were too tired and busy to respond to other messages coming in for the *Carpathia*.

Captain Rostron persuaded Bruce Ismay to send a telegram to the White Star offices in New York. The full message read: "Deeply regret advise you *Titanic* sank this morning after collision iceberg, resulting serious loss life. Full particulars later. Bruce Ismay."[83]

When the *Carpathia* stopped outside New York harbor to pick up the pilot, reporters and curious people waited to come aboard. But Captain Rostron barred them from his ship, fearing they would upset the survivors. As the *Carpathia* proceeded into the harbor, it stopped briefly at the White Star Line's offices to deliver thirteen *Titanic* lifeboats. These were what remained of the world's greatest luxury liner.

One of the lifeboats bearing Titanic *survivors is hoisted onto the* Carpathia. *The* Carpathia *searched the accident site for four hours and found only pieces of wreckage and dead bodies.*

7 How Could This Happen?

As the first wireless messages about the *Titanic* reached shore early Monday morning, most people chose not to believe them. Newspaper reporters in New York City hurried to the White Star office to verify rumors that the ship had sunk and people had been evacuated in lifeboats, but the line's officials could not yet tell them what had happened. Philip Franklin, vice president of the line, declared, "We place absolute confidence in the *Titanic*. We believe that the boat is unsinkable."[84]

Confusing Reports

During the trip to New York, the *Carpathia* refused to give out information. Captain Arthur Rostron limited the use of the wireless to messages from survivors and for official business. Newspaper headlines protested the lack of information, and false rumors circulated. Some reports stated that the ship had been damaged but did not sink; one said that all the passengers had been rescued and were being taken to Nova Scotia.

Crowds of curious people stood on the streets outside the offices of the *New York American* newspaper. There the newspaper's employees updated the news about the *Titanic* on a large chalkboard they had hung over the entrance to the building.

The *New York Times* was the first to risk publishing a report. Its front-page headlines on Monday, April 16 read: "TITANIC *SUNK FOUR HOURS AFTER HITTING ICEBERG; 866 RESCUED BY* CARPATHIA, *PROBABLY 1250 PERISH; ISMAY SAFE, MRS. ASTOR MAYBE, NOTED NAMES MISSING.*" Beneath the headlines was a photograph of the ship and another of Captain Edward Smith. In the story, which took up the first twelve pages of the newspaper, the *Times* published a partial list of survivors.

By Tuesday morning, the reports coming in were increasingly dismal. After he confirmed that the *Titanic* really had sunk, the White Star's Franklin was forced to inform the press, as well as the people who had come to the office to find out about their relatives on board. By evening, Franklin was acknowledging that there may have been "a number of lives lost"; at 9:00 P.M., he had admitted that there was a "horrible loss of life."[85]

Newspapers throughout the country carried front-page stories about the tragedy. People around the world expressed shock and sorrow. This was an extraordinary event in a world unaccustomed to such disasters. A young naval officer who was visiting New York City the night of April 16 wrote

"All the News That's Fit to Print."

The New York Times.

VOL. LXI...NO. 19,906.   NEW YORK, TUESDAY, APRIL 16, 1912.—TWENTY-FOUR PAGES.   ONE CENT

THE WEATHER.

TITANIC SINKS FOUR HOURS AFTER HITTING ICEBERG; 866 RESCUED BY CARPATHIA, PROBABLY 1250 PERISH; ISMAY SAFE, MRS. ASTOR MAYBE, NOTED NAMES MISSING

Col. Astor and Bride, Isidor Straus and Wife, and Maj. Butt Aboard.

"RULE OF SEA" FOLLOWED

Women and Children Put Over in Lifeboats and Are Supposed to be Safe on Carpathia.

PICKED UP AFTER 8 HOURS

Vincent Astor Calls at White Star Office for News of His Father and Leaves Weeping.

FRANKLIN HOPEFUL ALL DAY

Manager of the Line Insisted Titanic Was Unsinkable Even After She Had Gone Down.

HEAD OF THE LINE ABOARD

J. Bruce Ismay Making First Trip on Gigantic Ship That Was to Surpass All Others.

The Lost Titanic Being Towed Out of Belfast Harbor.

Biggest Liner Plunges to the Bottom at 2:20 A.M.

RESCUERS THERE TOO LATE

Except to Pick Up the Few Hundreds Who Took to the Lifeboats.

WOMEN AND CHILDREN FIRST

Cunarder Carpathia Rushing to New York with the Survivors.

SEA SEARCH FOR OTHERS

The Californ Stands By on Chance of Picking Up Other Boats or Rafts.

OLYMPIC SENDS THE NEWS

Only Ship to Flash Wireless Messages to Shore After the Disaster.

CAPT. E. J. SMITH, Commander of the Titanic.

PARTIAL LIST OF THE SAVED.

Includes Bruce Ismay, Mrs. Widener, Mrs. H. B. Harris, and an incomplete name, suggesting Mrs. Astor's.

The New York Times *headline announcing the* Titanic *disaster.*

The Musicians' Plight

All eight musicians aboard the *Titanic* went down with the ship. The two pianists had remained with their colleagues even after their instruments were washed away. As the ship neared its end, Wallace Hartley told the men to save themselves if they wished, but all eight remained and continued playing. After the disaster, they were widely praised. People from around the world sent sympathetic messages to their families.

In *The Night Goes On*, Walter Lord describes the problems these men and their families endured. Early in 1912, C. W. and F. N. Black had gained the exclusive right to provide all the musicians who worked on passenger ships. They told the steamship companies that their agency would charge less than what the companies had been paying directly to the musicians—the union rate of £6, 10 shillings a month and a uniform allowance. After all the lines had signed contracts with the Blacks, the shipboard musicians found themselves forced to work for the agency, and their pay dropped to £4 a month—with no uniform allowance. The steamship company gave them a token shilling every month so that they would still be considered crew and have to heed the captain's orders like any other crew members.

The musicians' union had tried in vain to improve this situation. In March 1912, the musicians working on the *Olympic* approached Bruce Ismay for help. Instead, Ismay told them that if their union did not want them to travel as crew members, they could be listed as passengers, Second Class. This then created new problems for the musicians, who were treated as passengers when the ship docked in New York and had to appear before immigration officials.

After the ship sank, the bereaved families thought they were entitled to workmen's compensation benefits from the White Star Line, but the company refused to pay them. The Black agency also denied any liability to compensate the families, as did the agency's insurance company. In vain, the musicians' union urged the White Star Line to accept a moral duty to pay the families. But the British courts upheld the decisions of the company and the Black agency.

Help for the musicians came in 1913 from the *Titanic* Relief Fund. People from all over the world had been donating money to help needy survivors and the families of people who died on the ship, and this fund was set up to manage those gifts. It was ultimately decided to give the musicians' families the same benefits as those of the crew members.

to his mother about what happened on the streets when the news broke:

> Crowds of people were coming out of the theaters, cafes were going full tilt, when the newsboys began to cry, "Extra! Extra! *Titanic* sunk with 1800 aboard!" You can't imagine the effect of those words on the crowd. Nobody could realize what had happened, and when they did begin to understand, the excitement was almost enough to cause a panic in the theaters. Women began to faint and weep, and scores of people in evening clothes jumped into cabs and taxis and rushed to the offices of the White Star Line, where they remained all night waiting for news.[86]

In cities all over Britain and the United States, flags were lowered to half-mast, and numerous social events were cancelled. People began to wonder whether the ship had been doomed from the start. They recalled the near collision between the *Titanic* and the *New York* as the *Titanic* was making its way downriver to sea, for example. There was renewed interest in an 1898 novel, *The Wreck of the Titan*, by U.S. author Morgan Robertson. In that novel a huge passenger ship called the *Titan* hit an iceberg in the North Atlantic and sank, despite claims that the vessel was unsinkable.

Arrival in New York

Despite heavy rains, more than thirty thousand people gathered in New York harbor and another ten thousand thronged the Battery at the tip of Manhattan to watch the *Carpathia* arrive on the night of April 18. Police had to order the mobs to disperse so the passengers could disembark in peace.

An exception was made for the man whose invention had saved many lives. Guglielmo Marconi was escorted into the *Carpathia* and taken to the wireless cabin, where radio operator Harold Bride sat, his feet thickly wrapped in bandages. Marconi shook the young man's hand.

*A newspaper boy holds a "*Titanic Disaster*" poster in the streets of New York. Many people lined up near the docks in Manhattan to see the* Carpathia *deliver the survivors.*

Crowds gather to read bulletins of the sinking of the Titanic *posted on the corner of the Sun Building in New York City.*

Outside, the noisy crowd clamored to see the passengers, shouting their names and pointing flash cameras as they disembarked. The survivors moved through the crowds, many into the arms of relatives who had come for them in limousines. Charity workers and clergymen were also on hand to aid and comfort people, especially immigrants or people traveling alone.

Some of the survivors spoke to the press. Harold Bride sold his story to the *New York Times*, which published it under the headlines *"745 SAW TITANIC SINK WITH 1595 HER BAND PLAYING. HIT ICEBERG AT 21 KNOTS AND TORE HER BOTTOM OUT. 'I'LL FOLLOW THE SHIP' LAST WORDS OF CAPT SMITH. MANY WOMEN STAYED TO PERISH WITH HUSBANDS."*[87]

A week passed before an official list of the *Titanic*'s survivors was available. Then it appeared in newspapers and was posted in hotel lobbies, theaters, and stores. New York newspapers paid special attention to the fate of the wealthiest passengers, including the Strauses, Archibald Butt, Benjamin Guggenheim, and the Astors.

"A Hoodoo Area"

Ships crossing the North Atlantic avoided the area where the *Titanic* had sunk. Captains were heard to say, "It's a hoodoo area. Best to keep the living away from the dead."[88] Steamship companies moved their lanes farther south to avoid the icebergs.

However, before these changes occurred, some ships passed by the tragic site. Still visible were deck chairs, a barber's striped pole, and other debris in the icy waters. A woman on board a passenger liner told members of the press in New York what she saw:

> We saw the body of one woman dressed only in her night dress and clasping a baby to her breast. Close by was the body of another woman with her arms tightly clasped round a shaggy dog. . . . We saw the bodies of three men in a group, all clinging to a chair. Floating by just beyond them were the bodies of a dozen men all wearing lifebelts and clinging desperately together as though in their last struggle for life.[89]

A Grim Task

After the *Titanic* sank, White Star officials chartered a small ship from Nova Scotia to look for bodies. They assumed that many of the dead would be floating, because they would have been wearing lifejackets.

On April 17, the *Mackay-Bennett* set out from Halifax with a clergyman and an undertaker on board. During a two-week search, 398 bodies were recovered and placed in coffins or cloth shrouds along the deck. A crew member recorded the gender, the estimated age, and the appearance of each corpse, along with its clothing, jewelry, and the contents of pockets. Badly decomposed bodies were buried at sea under the direction of the clergyman; 190 others were returned for burial on land.

"The Love of Our Hearts"

The 150 unclaimed bodies from the *Titanic* were buried in Halifax, Nova Scotia, in three cemeteries, according to religion: Protestant, Catholic, and Jewish. Among those interred were John Law Hume, the ship's violinist, and his fellow musician, bass player J. Fred Clarke. The tallest stone stands over the grave of a two-year-old child, the only child's body recovered by the crew of the *Mackay-Bennett.* The epitaph reads: "Erected to the memory of an unknown child whose remains were recovered after the disaster to the Titanic April 15th 1912."

The Maritime Museum in Halifax contains a deck chair from the *Titanic* that was recovered during the search for bodies. People wrote to officials in Halifax to inquire about their loved ones or to acknowledge receiving news of their burial. One of these letters, now in the museum, came from an elderly woman from Southampton. It was dated July 1912:

> Dear Sir. I have been informed by Mr F Blake Superintendent Engineer of the White Star Line Trafalgar Chambers on the 10th that the Body of my Beloved Son Herbert Jupe which was Electrical Engineer No. 3 on the Ill-Fatted Titanic has been recovered and Burried at Sea by the Cable Steamer "Mackey-Bennett" and that his Silver Watch and Handkerchief marked H.J. is in your Possesion. He bought him half a dox of the same when he was at Belfast with the R.M.S. Olympic to have a new blade put to one of her Perpellors we are extremely oblidged for all your Kindness to my Precious Boy. He was not married and was the Love of our Hearts and he loved his Home But God gave and God has taken Him Blessed be the Name of the Lord. He has Left an Aceing Void in our Home which cannot be filled.
>
> Please Send along the Watch and Handkerchief marked H.J.
>
> > Yours Truly C. Jupe
> > His Mother is 72 Last April 4th.
> > His Father is 68 Last Feb. 9th.

Among them was Colonel John Jacob (Jack) Astor's body. His pockets held twenty-five hundred dollars in cash and a gold watch, still ticking. The watch was given to twenty-year-old Vincent Astor, his son and primary heir, who treasured it all his life. A funeral was held in May. In his will, Jack Astor left a fortune worth more than $87 million.

After eight days, the *Mackay-Bennett* returned home and the *Minia* took up the quest. It recovered seventeen bodies and buried two at sea. Then two other ships joined the search, but they found only five more bodies. Flags in Halifax were flown at half-mast as the bodies were returned. Undertakers and embalmers received them in a building that had been set up as a temporary mortuary, where a coroner issued death certificates. Friends, relatives, and representatives arrived to identify and claim the bodies.

The *Algerine*, which went out to search on May 14, found just one body, that of saloon steward James McGrady, the last body recovered from the tragedy. Of 328 bodies, 128 remained unidentified.

Continuing Interest

The press continued to cover each new development in the *Titanic* disaster. Interviews with survivors filled newspapers and magazines. Many accounts contained exaggerations and lies. People also sought deeper meanings in the disaster, with some attacking the very existence of the great, luxurious ship.

The renowned author and veteran sailor Joseph Conrad wrote a scathing article called "Some Reflexions, Seamanlike and Otherwise" for the 1912 edition of the *English Review*. Of the victims, Conrad wrote, "To the last moment, they put their trust in mere bigness, in the reckless affirmations of commercial men and mere technicians and in the irresponsible paragraphs of the newspapers booming these ships."[90]

Clergymen delivered heated sermons about pride and greed. They criticized the profit-hungry shipping industry and the sins of the rich. A number of people regarded the disaster as a sign that humans must recognize their limitations and accept their inferiority to God. During a sermon at St. Mary's Church in England weeks after the sinking, the bishop of Winchester declared that the "*Titanic*, name and thing, will stand for a monument and warning to human presumption."[91]

Investigating the Tragedy

Only two days after the *Titanic* sank, the U.S. Senate began an investigation of it. Americans were outraged that so many people had died. In addition, because American financiers owned the White Star Line, Congress felt it a duty to find out what had happened and provide more safeguards for passengers at sea.

Senator William Alden Smith of Michigan chaired the subcommittee, which heard testimony from surviving passengers and crew members and people with specialized knowledge. Key witnesses included Bruce Ismay, director of the White Star Line, Captain Arthur Rostron of the *Carpathia*, and members of the *Titanic*'s crew, including Second Officer Lightoller, Fifth Officer Lowe, lookout Fred Fleet, and wireless operator Harold Bride. Survivors from the

First, Second, and Third Class sections also testified or sent in written affidavits.

For weeks, investigators asked people what had happened and why. For instance, why were there so few lifeboats on board? The witnesses explained that under British Board of Trade regulations, a ship of more than ten thousand tons needed to carry no more than sixteen lifeboats. This law seemed quite outdated for a ship like the *Titanic*, which weighed more than forty thousand tons and could accommodate 3,547 people.

Why did the ship not slow down after the captain and crew received several ice warnings? Was Captain Smith too casual or naive about the danger? Or was he determined to move at top speed despite the hazards posed by icebergs? Captain Smith had gone down with the ship, so nobody could ask him these questions. However, some speculated that he had kept the *Titanic* moving at high speeds to please Bruce Ismay, the White Star Line's director, who was on board. Smith may also have come to believe that his magnificent new ship was in fact unsinkable.

After Ismay testified that Smith had made all the decisions during that fateful night, some people criticized him for seeming to try to blame the dead captain. By this time, many people were directing their anger and scorn at Ismay, the most visible symbol of the sunken ship. The naval historian and rear admiral A. T. Mahan spoke for many when he told a reporter, "I hold that under the conditions, so long as there was a soul that could be saved, the obligation lay upon Mr Ismay that that one person and not he should have been in the boat."[92]

A rumor spread that Ismay had boarded a lifeboat before it was filled and had personally chosen crew members to row it. However, a witness testified that Ismay had entered the last boat that was fully launched, Collapsible Boat A, and that one of the *Titanic's* officers had urged him to get in, because no women and children remained on deck.

Further testimony revealed weaknesses in the ship's design and construction. For instance, the two strongest pumps were located in the engine rooms but would have been more effective in the boiler rooms. And the doors between the watertight compartments on the *Titanic* would have given more protection if they had gone one deck higher.

A set of the Titanic*'s engines under construction in the shipyard in 1911. After the ship sank, many wondered if its design and construction were flawed.*

A Long-Standing Debate

Both the American and the British inquest heard a great deal of testimony about the location and activities of the *Californian*. Had this ship been closer to the *Titanic* than the *Carpathia*? Did it see the signal rockets but ignore them?

After the *Californian* arrived in Boston harbor on April 19, Captain Stanley Lord explained why his ship had not heard the distress messages sent by wireless the preceding night. He also said that the *Californian* had had to dodge numerous icebergs on its way to the site of the disaster. Even in daylight, it had taken three full hours for the ship to make its way through the ice field.

For more than a week, little was written about the *Californian* and her whereabouts the night of the sinking. Then curious reporters probed more deeply and found out that Captain Lord had been sleeping after a long day at work and had not been on deck when the *Titanic*'s rockets were fired, which some crew members on the *Californian* said they had seen. People also wondered why the ship's scrap log (a rough record in which the officer on duty describes the weather, speed, course of the ship, and any sightings or unusual events) had vanished. The ship's regular log did not mention any distress rockets from the *Titanic*.

The U.S. Senate Committee concluded that the *Californian* was less than nineteen miles from the *Titanic*, saw the rockets, and "failed to respond to them in accordance with the dictates of humanity, international usage, and the requirements of law." The British inquest reached a similar conclusion, saying, "When she first saw the rockets, the *Californian* could have pushed through the ice to the open water without any serious risk and so have come to the assistance of the *Titanic*. Had she done so, she might have saved many if not all of the lives that were lost."

Captain Lord disputed these findings and received support from the Mercantile Marine Services Association as well as certain members of Parliament. Some supporters claimed that the *Titanic* had sent the *Californian* the wrong position or that the two ships had been separated by a wall of ice that could not be breached. In later years, new evidence showed that a third (and perhaps even a fourth) ship had also been in the region that night.

People speculated that the crew members had not received the proper training to operate this enormous ship. It was suggested that the captain and crew did not really know how long it would take the ship to stop or turn at different speeds. The *Titanic*'s sea trials had lasted a mere eight hours. Other liners had gone through several weeks of trials.

The public was amazed to hear that there had never been any lifeboat drills, and the lookouts did not have binoculars. It also came out that the wireless operators were often overworked. The operators on the *Californian* and other ships frequently worked alone, which meant they could not run their equipment twenty-four hours a day.

The British Investigation

As the U.S. inquest continued, a critical British press observed that unlike its chairman, Senator Smith, the British lead investigator, Lord Mersey, was an expert on nautical affairs. One writer for the *Daily Telegraph* (London) said that

> the inquiry which has been in progress in America has effectively illustrated the inability of the lay mind to grasp the problem of marine navigation. It is a matter of congratulation that British custom provides a more satisfactory method of investigating the circumstances attending a wreck.[93]

During a month-long inquest, Mersey heard testimony about the design of the ship, the outdated lifeboat regulations, and the speeds at which steamships traveled. The British investigators noted the total number of men, women, and children lost and saved in every class of the ship. In First Class, 118 men were lost and 57 survived; 4 women were lost and 140 survived; 1 child was lost and 6 survived. In Second Class, 154 men were lost and 14 survived; 13 women were lost and 80 survived; no children were lost and all 24 survived. In Third Class, 387 men were lost and 75 survived; 89 women were lost and 76 survived; 52 children were lost and 27 survived. Of the crew members, 670 men were lost and 192 survived; 3 women crew members were lost and 20 survived.

Clearly, a higher percentage of Third Class passengers died. Had these people been treated fairly, or had they been ignored or even barred from reaching the lifeboats? Witnesses, including Third Class survivors, said that the women and children had been placed in lifeboats without regard to their class. The door connecting the Third Class companionway to the Second Class staircase was opened after the accident, not locked. The crew was told to bring women up from the steerage compartment at 12:30 A.M. when the lifeboats were being loaded. Steward John Hart testified that many of the Third Class women would not get into the lifeboats and some even refused to wear lifejackets.[94] Many also refused to leave their husbands.

Neither of the inquests concluded that any steerage passengers had been forcibly prevented from reaching the boat deck. However, the crew may have failed to find some of the Third Class passengers, because they did not systematically search the cabins and public rooms in the steerage section. It also seemed that the Third Class passengers were not informed as quickly as others about the impending disaster.

Only two survivors testified before Lord Mersey's committee: Sir Cosmo and

*These children were two of the lucky ones. One hundred ten children were
on the* Titanic *when it sank. More than half of them perished.*

Lady (Lucile) Duff-Gordon. The couple and
Lady Duff Gordon's secretary had been on
board Lifeboat One. This boat was given
over to only twelve people, which sparked
many questions and criticisms. Although
the Duff-Gordons were cleared of any misconduct, they were later ostracized by some
in their social circle.

Critical Reports

In the end, the two inquests produced
more than two thousand pages of testimony. These records have been widely read
by scientific researchers, historians, writers,
and other interested people.

The report issued by Senator Smith
and his committee criticized Captain Smith
for being overconfident and indifferent to
danger. The committee said that lifeboat
drills should have been held and that the
escape from the ship was disorganized. In
addition to the lifeboats leaving the *Titanic*
unfilled, they lacked adequate supplies and
compasses. Only three contained lamps.
The committee also concluded that the
steerage passengers died in higher numbers than First and Second Class passengers because they were not informed of the
danger as soon as the others. The inquest

recommended that each ship hire enough wireless operators to keep the radios going day and night.

Author Walter Lord, who wrote two best-selling books about the disaster, concluded that "given the competitive pressures of the North Atlantic run, the chances taken, the lack of experience with ships of such immense size, the haphazard procedures of the wireless room, the casualness of the bridge, and the misassessment of what speed was safe, it's remarkable that the *Titanic* steamed for two hours and ten minutes through ice-infested waters without coming to grief any sooner."[95]

New Laws to Protect Passengers

As a result of this disaster, an international meeting on the subject of Safety of Life at Sea met in London in November 1913 and January 1914. The group agreed on the necessity for new laws regarding lifeboats, safe speeds, communication systems, and related matters. They moved the standard southern route in the North Atlantic farther south to lessen the chances of ships' encountering ice.

As a result of these meetings, the International Ice Patrol was formed to spot ice in the North Atlantic and provide maps showing hazardous areas. The nations using the North Atlantic, including Britain, the United States, the Netherlands, Germany, Canada, France, Belgium, Israel, Italy, Japan, Sweden, Poland, and Greece, contributed to its operation.

The International Ice Patrol was eventually moved to Groton, Connecticut, after it ultimately came under the direction of the U.S. Coast Guard. Using aircraft with radar, patrol officers now monitor iceberg movements and broadcast this information. No lives have been lost because of icebergs since 1912 in the area covered by the Ice Patrol. Yet ships have sunk after striking icebergs in other areas. In 1959 the *Hans Hedtoft* sank after hitting a berg off the coast of Greenland. Ninety-five passengers and crew died in that accident.

One Ice Patrol publication has called icebergs a "natural hazard which man, in all his ingenuity and resourcefulness, has not been able to control, regulate, or entirely avoid."[96] The U.S. Navy once conducted experiments to find ways to destroy large icebergs but found them to be nearly indestructible (nearly two thousand tons of explosives are needed to break up an average-sized iceberg). Historians believe that the iceberg the *Titanic* hit was small to medium in size, standing fifty to one hundred feet above the water. It may have weighed about half a million tons. Icebergs weighing several million tons have been found in the North Atlantic.

In 1915, the U.S. Congress passed the Smith bill, which required every vessel carrying more than fifty passengers to carry a wireless set with a range of at least one hundred miles. Wireless rooms must be kept running twenty-four hours a day, and operators now receive better pay and have improved working conditions. Seamen's rights were also strengthened in the La Follette Seaman's Act of 1915.

All nations are now expected to make sure that experienced crews are on board and that lifeboat drills are carried out. Each passenger or crew member must have a specific seat in a lifeboat, which must have room for every person on board, and ships' crews must be trained to use the boats.

Changes have also been made in how ships are built. They must now have stronger keels (bottoms), which require new kinds of hulls. Bulkheads have been strengthened, pumping equipment improved. Before these new regulations came in, the White Star Line had already strengthened the bulkheads on the *Titanic*'s sister ship, the *Olympic*, and had placed more lifeboats on board. The *Olympic* would serve as a passenger ship until the early 1930s.

Legal Battles

Numerous lawsuits were filed against the White Star Line and the owners of the *Titanic*, with some claims not being settled for years. The insurance syndicate paid out $420,000 dollars for the lost contents of the ship's hold, but individual passengers had also lost valuables. A rare edition of *The Rubaiyat of Omar Khayyam* had been on board. The book's binding was studded with more than a thousand precious gems. Other passengers lost gold coins, currency, and fine jewelry.

The claims varied greatly. Mrs. Charlotte Cardeza of Philadelphia filed suit for $177,352.74 in lost property; Eugene Daly claimed $50 for his lost bagpipes. William Carter submitted a claim for the new Renault he had brought, worth $5,000. Others sought compensation for lost photographs, books, a prize bulldog, or oil paintings.

People also demanded financial compensation for the loss of family members. The largest single claim, for $1 million, was filed by René Harris, widow of the theatrical producer Henry B. Harris, who claimed that her loss of his creative talent caused her enormous financial hardship. The families of the wealthiest passengers who had drowned did not file monetary claims against the White Star Line, perhaps because they thought it would be undignified.

As the cases were being filed, both in the United States and Britain, attorneys for the claimants argued that the ship had been handled with negligence and that Bruce Ismay, the line's director, had been aware of danger but had influenced the captain to go too fast.

The two sides reached an agreement out of court in August 1916. The White Star Line paid out $665,000, a small percentage of the amount the claimants had asked for, which totaled more than $16 million. In response the claimants agreed to drop their lawsuits.

By 1916 the legal issues had subsided and new laws were in place, but the public remained interested in stories about the *Titanic* and the fate of its 705 survivors.

Chapter

8 Unending Fascination

The subject of the *Titanic* has emerged again and again since 1912. During the weeks, months, and years immediately after the ship sank, people continued to follow newspaper accounts of the legal battles fought by her survivors and the new laws that were passed to protect passengers at sea.

Most absorbing of all were the human stories. People were curious about those who had survived the terrifying night when so many lives were changed and heroes and legends born.

Changed Lives

More than any other community, Southampton, England, the starting point of the fateful journey, was devastated by the *Titanic* tragedy. Many of the crew members came from this port and Captain Edward Smith had also lived there. One local newspaper published a photograph of forty young children from one school who had each lost a father, a brother, or an uncle. On one street alone near the docks, the residents

This is the monument erected to the people lost on the Titanic *in Southampton, England. Many of the ship's crew were from Southampton, including Captain Smith.*

Millvina Dean, 86, is one of the few living Titanic *survivors. She was only nine weeks old at the time and though her brother and mother also survived, her father, Bertram, did not.*

had lost a total of thirteen family members. Seven memorials were built in Southampton to honor the engineers and other seamen who had died on the *Titanic*.

A memorial was also built in New York, for Isidor and Ida Straus. Although the Strauses had made a fortune in the department store business, they had not lived lavishly and had given a great deal of money to charity. Forty thousand New Yorkers attended a memorial service at a Jewish temple for this heroic couple. A small park in a section of the city where Isidor had once operated a little dairy farm was dedicated in their memory. Macy's department store employees contributed to the plaque for one of the entrances. When the Strauses' maid tried to return Mrs. Straus's fur coat, their daughter urged her to keep it as a gift.

Other survivors honored their own lost relatives. In the name of her son Harry, Mrs. George Widener donated a library, which still bears his name, to Harvard University. And the New York Public Library received the rare books Jack Astor had collected during his lifetime.

People heard that the *Titanic*'s youngest survivor was nine-week-old Millvina Dean. She and her eighteen-month-old brother and her mother Georgetta had been saved in the lifeboats, but her father, Bertram, was lost. In America, a new home awaited them in the Midwest, where Bertram had planned to open a tobacco shop. They had first been booked on a different liner, which did not depart on schedule because of a coal strike. After the family was offered passage on the great new ship leaving April 12, Mr. Dean told his family, "Isn't it wonderful that we've been asked to go on the *Titanic*?"[97]

When Mrs. Dean and her two young children were rescued and reached New York, they were sent back to England, to live with Georgetta's parents for eight years. Donations from the Titanic Survivors' Fund kept them going until Georgetta remarried. Millvina later recalled that her mother suffered for years from headaches and other signs of stress after the disaster at sea.[98]

After writing a firsthand account, Archibald Gracie died, nine months after the *Titanic* sank, from the effects of his ordeal. His shipboard friend, the author Helen Churchill Candee published a book on tapestry in 1913. She later became a well-known travel lecturer specializing in Asian countries. Candee died at the age of ninety in Maine.

René Harris received only $50,000 of the $1 million she had sought in her lawsuit against the White Star Line. She used the money to finance plays at the theater she and her husband operated in New York. Harris successfully produced new plays throughout the 1920s.

Two couples who met aboard the *Titanic* later married. They were the widow of Lucien P. Smith, who married Robert Daniel; and Karl Behr, who married Helen Newsom. Behr became a well-known tennis player, as did his fellow survivor twenty-one-year-old Richard Norris (Dick) Williams, who lost his father when the ship sank. When he was rescued, Williams's legs were so frostbitten that the doctors advised their amputation. Williams refused, recovered, and later won numerous major titles, including U.S. men's singles champion in 1914, 1915, and 1916.

The officers who survived the sinking of the *Titanic* were never given the chance to command their own ships. Perhaps the White Star Line feared they would remind passengers of the tragedy. Second Officer Herbert Lightoller, who was thirty-eight years old in 1912, did command a destroyer for the Royal Naval Reserve in World War I. He retired as chief officer on the *Celtic* in the early 1920s. However, he continued to love sailing his own yacht and was among the brave civilians who took part in a daring rescue during World War II. In 1940, Allied soldiers were stranded on a French beach at Dunkirk after losing a battle against German troops. Fishing boats and other private vessels saved thousands of Allies from capture or death. Lightoller rescued 131 of them in his *Sundowner*.

Pressure forced Bruce Ismay to retire in 1913 as chairman of the White Star Line. In the years that followed, he lived quietly out of the public eye until he died of a stroke in 1937.

The White Star Line launched the *Titanic*'s sister ship *Britannic* in 1914. Two years later, it was sunk by enemy fire during World War I. Amazingly, Violet Jessop, a stewardess who had survived the *Titanic* disaster, was on board this ship when it also sank. She survived a second time.

The White Star Line never recovered its former reputation after the *Titanic*. By the 1930s, the company was declining. It eventually merged with the Cunard Line to become the Cunard White Star Line, which finally became simply the Cunard Line. Larger ships were coming into existence. During the 1920s, two fabulous German ocean liners were launched: the *Bremen* and the *Europa*. Within a decade,

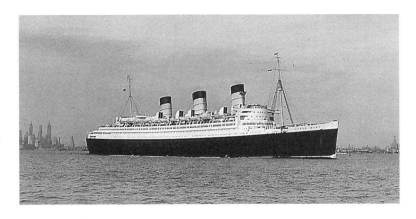

The White Star Line began a slow decline after the Titanic *tragedy. Bigger and more luxurious ships, like the* Queen Mary, *eclipsed its own and it eventually merged with the Cunard Line.*

the *Normandie* (French) and the *Queen Mary* (British), two ships even larger and more luxurious, were launched.

Renewed Interest

Interest in the *Titanic* waned but was revived with the 1955 publication of Walter Lord's dramatic book *A Night to Remember*. Books, plays, musicals, and theatrical and television films continued to interest new generations. By 1998, seven motion pictures had been made about the disaster. A Broadway musical, *The Unsinkable Molly Brown*, included scenes that showed Brown aboard the *Titanic* and surviving in a lifeboat afterward. In 1960 the musical reached larger audiences when it was made into a popular feature film starring Debbie Reynolds.

Three years later in 1963, people with a strong interest in the *Titanic* formed the Titanic Historical Society. The society, which steadily gained members, published a magazine and gathered *Titanic* relics, mostly from survivors. It donated them to a permanent exhibit at the Philadelphia Maritime Museum.

Why does the *Titanic* continue to fascinate people? Historian John Maxtone-Graham says that the story combines "wonder, splendor, hubris, tragedy, and death in one imperishable package."[99] Author Walter Lord points out that the *Titanic* was a major news event: "The biggest ship in the world, proclaimed unsinkable, hits an iceberg on her maiden voyage and goes down, taking with her many of the best-known celebrities of the day."[100] In addition, says Lord, the story holds many "if onlys":

If only she had paid more attention to the warnings she received . . . if only the last warning had even reached the bridge . . . if only the wireless operator hadn't cut off one final attempt to reach her . . . if only she had sighted the ice a few seconds sooner, or a few seconds later . . . if only there had been enough lifeboats . . . if only the water-tight bulkheads had gone one deck higher . . . if only that ship on the horizon had come . . . if only, if only.[101]

The sinking itself presented unanswered questions that also captured people's interest. Had the ship sunk intact, or had it broken up before it sank? The eyewitnesses' accounts differed. Sixteen of twenty people who described the sinking believed the ship had split as it went into the water. And exactly what had happened to the side of the ship when it hit the iceberg? These and other mysteries would remain unsolved for more than seventy years.

Deep-Sea Exploration

After the *Titanic* sank, people wondered about the ship itself and longed to explore its wreckage that lay deep in the North Atlantic. By 1914 several people had proposed ways to lift the wreckage out of the ocean. One of these plans involved a submarine equipped with electromagnets and cables.

Interest waned during World War I and again in the 1930s, when a severe economic depression gripped the world. That crisis was followed by another devastating world war. However, during the 1950s, publication of Walter Lord's popular book

A Megahit Movie

The dramatic story of the *Titanic* has inspired many books, poems, songs, plays, and films. *Atlantic*, a play about the sinking, was made into a movie in 1930. A German film about the *Titanic*, made during World War II, featured a fictional German officer who was made into the "hero" of the disaster. In Twentieth Century Fox's 1953 film *Titanic*, several well-known actors portrayed fictional characters. Three years later, large audiences tuned in for a television production based on Walter Lord's 1955 book, *A Night to Remember*. By popular demand, this program was broadcast twice in a five-week period. Lord's book was then made into a movie, released in 1958. The year 1979 brought a television movie, *S.O.S. Titanic*. In 1980 the subject reappeared in movie theaters when *Raise the Titanic*, based on a Clive Cussler novel of the same name, was released.

The 1997 feature film *Titanic* was the most expensive of the movies made about this maritime disaster. This fact-based film portrayed many of the real-life passengers. Several of the main characters were invented, however, and the main story line involved a fictional romance between Jack (an artist traveling in steerage, played by Leonardo di Caprio) and Rose (a socialite in First Class, played by Kate Winslet). With its spectacular special effects and popular musical score, *Titanic* became the largest grossing film of all time, passing the $1.6 billion mark in 1998. The film received eleven Academy Awards, tying the all-time record set by the 1959 film *Ben Hur*. Throughout the world, people have been moved by the story and have seen the film in record numbers.

sparked new interest in the idea of finding the *Titanic*.

People have traditionally explored the ocean in order to find treasure or for scientific or historical reasons. Those who wanted to explore for the *Titanic* were motivated more by historic and scientific goals, as well as a desire simply to accomplish this amazing feat. The ship's cargo list did not mention any items of tremendous value that would likely remain intact after the sinking.

Although people had explored the sea for centuries, they made ever steadier progress after about 1800. Scientists began studying the tides and tried to estimate the depths of the ocean throughout the world using new kinds of instruments. They learned more and more about the thousands of plants and animals that inhabited

"Fascinated by the Sea"

Robert D. Ballard led the research teams that successfully located the *Titanic* and explored the ship a year later. In his book *Exploring the Titanic* (1989), he wrote, "As long as I can remember I've been fascinated by the sea." Ballard grew up in southern California, where he learned to scuba dive and his favorite book was *20,000 Leagues Under the Sea*, by Jules Verne. While studying marine geology at the University of Hawaii, Ballard worked as a porpoise and dolphin trainer at a local marine-life park.

Ballard headed for the East Coast in 1967 to begin service in the U.S. Navy, which had assigned him to work at the Woods Hole Oceanographic Institution in Falmouth, Massachusetts. There he joined a group called the Boston Sea Rovers, who shared his love of deep-sea exploration. The Rovers hosted famous speakers, including deep-sea diver Jacques Cousteau and shark expert Dr. Eugenie Clark, at their meetings.

During those years, Ballard began to hope that someday he would be able to explore the remains of the *Titanic*, even though experts said the ship had sunk so deep it was not accessible to explorers.

In 1973, Ballard became part of a three-man team that worked with a small submersible called the *Alvin*, built in 1966. The navy had given it a new hull made of a titanium alloy, so that it could withstand more underwater pressure, allowing it to plunge to depths of thirteen thousand feet. This reinforcement process was called Project Titanus. As Ballard described it:

> Titanium, Titanus, *Titanic*—that started me thinking. The *Titanic* was thought to lie at a depth of just over 12,000 feet. I suddenly realized that I could dive to the *Titanic* in *Alvin*. Now thoughts of the *Titanic* just wouldn't leave me alone. I knew that I had to find that ship.

During the 1970s, Ballard explored the Mid-Atlantic Ridge, the coast of Ecuador, and the waters off Baja California, among other places. He continued to think about ways to find the *Titanic* and sought out people who might finance such an expedition. Ballard's dream finally came true in 1985.

the seas. During the late 1880s, scientists found ways to bring up samples of materials from deep in the ocean. To this end Britain sponsored a major, four-year-long expedition aboard the *Challenger*, starting in 1872.

During the early 1900s, new equipment enabled oceanographers to move to lower depths and make even more precise maps of the ocean floor. They used special cameras, thermometers, pressure meters, and seismographs in this work. By 1930 scientists could take a vessel called a submersible down more than one thousand feet below the ocean's surface.

New and improved submersibles made deep-sea exploration safer after the 1960s. Better techniques and equipment were developed. Several prominent oceanographers then began to talk about locating and exploring the wreckage of the *Titanic*, which they believed had sunk to a depth of about two and a half miles. However, such an expedition would be very costly and would require the most sophisticated equipment.

Several parties made specific plans to try to raise the ship rather than explore it underwater. One such scheme involved attaching canvas bags to the hull, then pumping them full of hydrogen gas. The gas would pull up the hull to the surface, argued John Pierce, who devised this scheme. Later he proposed wrapping the remains of the ship in a net, into which he would pump nitrogen, which is lighter than seawater. Pierce thought the ship would rise after the nitrogen froze, but he could not find the financial backers to try out these plans.

Several expeditions tried to find the ship but failed. One of the most persistent explorers was an Englishman named Douglas Woolley. Although he was not a scientist or a financier, he had spent years reading about the *Titanic*. He came up with a plan to raise the ship using plastic bags filled with some eighty-five thousand cubic yards of hydrogen gas produced by the electrolysis of seawater. However, chemists said it might take years to produce so much hydrogen. In the end Woolley, like Pierce, was unable to assemble the investors or equipment he needed to try out his scheme.

Others continued to dream of finding the *Titanic*. Several groups made plans for such an expedition during the 1970s but faced a shortage of funding and other obstacles, including the lack of a suitable salvage vessel. In addition, the exact location of the wreckage remained uncertain. Finding it would be quite difficult in the rough waters of that region.

Jack Grimm, a wealthy Texas businessman, came close to finding the wreckage during the early 1980s. He spent $2 million on three separate attempts to locate the *Titanic*, aided by the Lamont-Doherty Geological Observatory at Columbia University and the Scripps Institution of Oceanography on the first two expeditions, in 1980 and 1981. With a group from Columbia University he also failed in July 1983.

"That's It!"

In 1985, the Woods Hole [Massachusetts] Oceanographic Institution, which is operated by the U.S. Navy, and the French government sponsored a new search. The National Geographic Society and the National Science Foundation helped make the expedition possible. The cost has since been estimated at $6 to $15 million.

The French research team set out first, in the vessel *Le Suroit*. On board was Dr. Robert D. Ballard, leader of the American group that would later operate the 245-foot research ship *Knorr*. The forty-two-year-old Ballard, a marine geologist and geophysicist, was head of the Woods Hole Deep Submergence Laboratory.

Before they left, the scientists and crew studied many pictures of the *Titanic*. During the early summer, *Le Suroit* surveyed about 80 percent of the area where the team expected to locate the sunken ship. They used a new type of side-scanning sonar named SAR (*Sonar Acoustique Remorqué*) that could reveal sections of sea-

The remote-controlled submersible, ARGO, was used to find the Titanic's *final resting place. It lies more than two and a half miles beneath the North Atlantic.*

floor three-fifths of a mile wide at one time. According to author Walter Lord, the SAR equipment allowed the crew to "cover as much ground in 20 days as previously took 12 years."[102]

However, six weeks passed but the team saw no trace of the ship. Ballard knew that in a few more weeks the usual bad autumn weather was due to hit the northwest Atlantic. He later wrote that "my dream of finding the *Titanic* was turning out to be a constant fight against time and nature."[103]

In August, Jean Jarry, the director of the French team, and two of his colleagues joined the American team on the *Knorr*. That vessel carried its own new technology in the form of the *Argo*, a deep-towed submersible about as big as a medium-sized car. The *Argo* contained a video system with five cameras pointing in different directions, along with intricate sonar and lighting and timing devices. The scientists would be able to steer the submersible and send back photographs from the ship.

The first eight days were frustrating. No signs of the *Titanic* were spotted among the miles of mud and sand dunes that moved across the video screen in the ship's control room. Shortly after midnight on September 1, however, something different passed by. The group in the control room glimpsed objects that looked to be of human origin. Then, around 1:00 A.M., they saw a huge object that they identified as one of the *Titanic*'s boilers.

Ballard was awakened and he rushed into the control room. Looking at the screen, he cried, "That's it!"[104] Other people on board hurried in to celebrate this triumphant moment. Around two o'clock, people realized that it was close to the time when the *Titanic* had sunk. The group then gathered on its stern, where they raised a Harland & Wolff flag and paid their respects to the fifteen hundred people who had perished on it.

For four days, the research group studied the site. They noted that the *Titanic* lay ten miles farther east than most people had thought. Ballard concluded that the navigator had miscalculated the ship's position when the distress messages were being sent. The ship's stern was in pieces, scattered more than a mile behind the wreck. By carefully maneuvering robot submersibles equipped with television cameras, the scientists were able to photograph the wreck and the surrounding area, taking more than twenty thousand frames of color film.

After the *Knorr* returned, Ballard spoke at a press conference in Washington, D.C.:

> The *Titanic* lies in 13,000 feet of water on a gently sloping alpine-like countryside overlooking a small canyon below. Its bow faces north and the ship sits upright on the bottom. Its mighty stacks pointing upward. There is no light at this great depth and little light can be found. It is quiet and peaceful and a fitting place for the remains of this greatest of sea tragedies to rest. May it forever remain that way and may God bless these souls.[105]

Inside the *Titanic*

In July 1986, fifty-six researchers from Woods Hole set out aboard the *Atlantis II*. The U.S. Navy had agreed to fund this new *Titanic* expedition, which cost about $220,000. Ballard and two other American

A set of breakfast dishes lies among the wreckage of the Titanic. *Experts estimate that it took over two hours for the massive ship to finally reach the ocean floor.*

oceanographers returned to the bottom in a submersible called the *Alvin*. It took about two and a half hours for it to reach the site where the *Titanic* lay, in dark, freezing-cold water. Along the way, they encountered sharks and many hazards. The crew moved cautiously, paying close attention to their equipment and surroundings.

Once they reached the site, the scientists studied the wreckage for eleven days. With a camera-equipped, deep-diving robot called Jason Junior ("*JJ*") they took more than sixty thousand high-resolution color photographs, as well as video pictures. The 250-pound *JJ* was tethered to the *Alvin* by a cable 250 feet long and was operated by remote control.

At first, *JJ* was used to photograph the external wreckage, which contained an immense amount of rust. Then, on the third day, operator Martin Bowen moved *JJ* inside the ship. In the area that was once the Grand Ballroom, the robot photographed the crystal chandelier and the remains of the Grand Staircase. No wood remained.

The bow of the Titanic *marks the final resting place of all those who went to the ocean floor with her. Many feel the ship is a hallowed site and should not be disturbed by salvage operations.*

Scientists guessed that marine organisms—mostly wood-eating worms—had eaten the nonmetallic parts of the wreckage.

Some mysteries were cleared up during this visit. It seemed that the ship had indeed broken apart during the sinking. The break occurred just in front of the *Titanic*'s third funnel. Also, people had once thought that the collision with the iceberg had caused a 300-foot-long gash along the hull, but Ballard's team found only intermittent punctures. The metal sheeting on the hull was ripped and bent, which would have allowed water to enter the interior compartments.

Graveyard or Salvage Site?

Ballard's team brought home hours of videotape and striking photographs of the *Titanic*, which were studied and published widely in books and magazines. Ballard said he hoped people would not disturb the site, which he called "hallowed ground." He said that visiting and photographing the wreckage had convinced him that "it would be wrong to attempt recovery of any of the remains. A photograph . . . is more powerful than the recovery of a single shoe; it is a statement in itself, a statement that describes a tragic, frozen moment in time."[106] Ballard asked the U.S. Congress to designate the *Titanic* an International Memorial so that it would be illegal to remove pieces of the ship or its contents from the site.

However, in the summer of 1987, a group of French explorers, supported by U.S. and Swiss investors, returned to collect artifacts from the *Titanic*. These salvaged items, including jewelry, china, statuary, and coins, were displayed in Paris in September 1987 and have since been shown around the world. Critics have said that it is immoral to remove and display objects from the *Titanic*, especially for profit. Survivor Eva Hart called this "an act of piracy."[107] She also argued that "the grave should be left alone."[108]

People continue to debate who "owns" the wreckage of the *Titanic* and how the site should be treated. Some say there are valid reasons to examine and display these items;

others feel the *Titanic* is a gravesite that should remain undisturbed for all time.

A Decisive Event

The *Titanic* tragedy continues to touch the minds and hearts of each generation. Partly this is because it remains the worst maritime disaster ever to occur during peacetime. Besides the terrible loss of life and the pain suffered by the survivors, families, and communities involved, the disaster stunned people around the world. This wondrous creation, the world's largest ship, had been built and launched with great confidence. It stood as a proud symbol of human achievement, another step on the road of steady progress.

Now it was gone, the "unsinkable" *Titanic*, struck down by the forces of nature.

Some of the world's richest, most powerful people had gone down with it. Was anyone really safe? What might happen next? Such doubts eroded people's feelings of security. In Newport, Rhode Island, poet Blanche Oelrichs (using a pen name, Michael Strange) wrote that the disaster "came as if some great stage manager planned that there would be a minor warning, a flash of horror" to prepare people for the turbulent times that loomed ahead.[109]

A survivor, Jack Thayer, later wrote that "it seems to me that the disaster . . . was the event which not only made the world rub its eyes and awake, but woke it with a start."[110] The next decade would bring many social and economic changes as well. Class distinctions would be challenged. Wars and revolutions would redraw national boundaries and alter the political landscape. Technology would continue to speed up the pace of life. A new era had begun.

Notes

Introduction: "Ship of Dreams"

1. Robert D. Ballard, *Exploring the Titanic.* New York: Madison, 1989, p. 57.

2. Quoted in William Hoffman and Jack Grimm, *Beyond Reach: The Search for the Titanic.* New York: Beaufort, 1982, p. 19.

3. Michael Davie, *Titanic: The Death and Life of a Legend.* New York: Knopf, 1987, p. 161.

Chapter 1: Twenty-Five Thousand Tons of Steel

4. Quoted in Hoffman and Grimm, *Beyond Reach*, p. 15.

5. Quoted in Davie, *Titanic*, p. 16.

6. Quoted in John P. Eaton and Charles A. Haas, *Titanic: Destination Disaster, the Legends and the Reality.* New York: Norton, 1987, p. 59.

7. Quoted in Geoffrey Marcus, *The Maiden Voyage.* New York: Viking, 1969, p. 80.

8. Marcus, *The Maiden Voyage*, p. 80.

9. Quoted in Hoffman and Grimm, *Beyond Reach*, p. 51.

10. Quoted in Hoffman and Grimm, *Beyond Reach*, p. 54.

11. Quoted in Hoffman and Grimm, *Beyond Reach*, p. 54.

Chapter 2: All Aboard!

12. Quoted in Don Lynch, *Titanic: An Illustrated History.* Toronto: Madison, 1992, p. 33.

13. Violet Jessop with John Maxtone-Graham, ed., *Titanic Survivor.* Dobbs Ferry, NY: Sheridan House, 1997, p. 10.

14. Marcus, *The Maiden Voyage*, p. 97.

15. Jessop with Maxtone-Graham, *Titanic Survivor*, p. 117.

16. Jessop with Maxtone-Graham, *Titanic Survivor*, p. 117.

17. From Lawrence F. Abbot, *The Letters of Archie Butt.* Garden City, New York: Doubleday Page, 1924, p. xxvi. Quoted in Marcus, *The Maiden Voyage*, p. 73.

18. Quoted in Davie, *Titanic*, p. 35.

19. Quoted in Shan F. Bullock, *A Titanic Hero: Thomas Andrews, Shipbuilder.* Riverside, CT: 7 C's Press, 1912. Reprint 1973, p. 63.

Chapter 3: "Nothing to Mar Our Pleasure"

20. Tom Kuntz, ed., *The Titanic Disaster Hearings: The Official Transcripts of the 1912 Senate Investigation.* New York: Pocket Books, 1998, p. 486.

21. Washington Dodge, *The Loss of the "Titanic."* Riverside, CT: 7C's Press, 1912, p. 4.

22. Quoted in Hoffman and Grimm, *Beyond Reach*, p. 53.

23. Quoted in Ballard, *Exploring the Titanic*, p. 14.

24. Quoted in Hoffman and Grimm, *Beyond Reach*, p. 63.

Chapter 4: Warning!

25. "Report on the Loss of the *Titanic*" (transcripts of British inquest), published in *Titanic: The Official Story, April 14–15, 1912*, p. 26.

26. Archibald Gracie, *Titanic: A Survivor's Story.* Chicago: Academy, 1913. Reprint 1986, p. 3.

27. Quoted in Davie, *Titanic*, p. 31.

28. Gracie, *Titanic*, p. 3.

29. Quoted in Hoffman and Grimm, *Beyond Reach*, p. 17.

30. Quoted in Kuntz, *The Titanic Disaster Hearings*, pp. 486–87.

31. Quoted in "Report on the Loss of the *Titanic*," p. 29.

32. Quoted in Eaton and Haas, *Titanic*, p. 13.

33. Jessop with Maxtone-Graham, *Titanic Survivor*, p. 124.

34. Quoted in Marcus, *The Maiden Voyage*, p. 127.

35. Quoted in Walter Lord, *The Night Lives On*. New York: William Morrow, 1986, p. 69.

36. Quoted in Kuntz, *The Titanic Disaster Hearings*, p. 177.

37. Quoted in Marcus, *The Maiden Voyage*, p. 130.

Chapter 5: To the Boats!

38. Quoted in Lynch, *Titanic*, p. 92.

39. Quoted in Kuntz, *The Titanic Disaster Hearings*, p. 85.

40. Quoted in Lynch, *Titanic*, p. 108.

41. Quoted in Eaton and Haas, *Titanic*, p. 21.

42. Quoted in Eaton and Haas, *Titanic*, p. 21.

43. Quoted in Davie, *Titanic*, p. 95.

44. Quoted in Kuntz, *The Titanic Disaster Hearings*, p. 482.

45. Quoted in Lynch, *Titanic*, p. 96.

46. Quoted in Hoffman and Grimm, *Beyond Reach*, p. 21.

47. Quoted in Kuntz, *The Titanic Disaster Hearings*, p. 491.

48. Quoted in Jessop with Maxtone-Graham, *Titanic Survivor*, p. 126.

49. Jessop with Maxtone-Graham, *Titanic Survivor*, p. 126.

50. Jessop with Maxtone-Graham, *Titanic Survivor*, p. 129.

51. Quoted in Hoffman and Grimm, *Beyond Reach*, p. 23.

52. Quoted in Eaton and Haas, *Titanic*, p. 27.

53. Quoted in Virginia Cowles, *The Astors*. New York: Knopf, 1979, p. 143.

54. Charles H. Lightoller, *Titanic and Other Ships*. London: Nicholson and Watson, 1935, pp. 233–34.

55. Jessop with Maxtone-Graham, *Titanic Survivor*, p. 132.

56. Gracie, *Titanic*, pp. 47–48.

57. Quoted in Gracie, *Titanic*, p. 45.

58. Gracie, *Titanic*, pp. 44–45.

59. Gracie, *Titanic*, pp. 44–45.

60. Quoted in Kuntz, *The Titanic Disaster Hearings*, p. 410.

61. Quoted in Davie, *Titanic*, p. 147.

Chapter 6: Terrifying Hours

62. Quoted in Davie, *Titanic*, p. 74.

63. Quoted in Davie, *Titanic*, p. 76.

64. Quoted in Davie, *Titanic*, p. 76.

65. Quoted in Anthony Masters, *Heroic Stories*. New York: Kingfisher, 1994, p. 50.

66. Quoted in Davie, *Titanic*, p. 77.

67. Quoted in Kuntz, *The Titanic Disaster Hearings*, p. 488.

68. Quoted in Masters, *Heroic Stories*, pp. 50–51.

69. Gracie, *Titanic*, p. 72.

70. Gracie, *Titanic*, p. 75.

71. Quoted in Lord, *The Night Lives On*, p. 153.

72. Quoted in Eaton and Haas, *Titanic*, p. 35.

73. Quoted in Davie, *Titanic*, pp. 78–79.

74. Quoted in Kuntz, *The Titanic Disaster Hearings*, pp. 428–29.

75. Gracie, *Titanic*, p. 95.

76. Quoted in Eaton and Haas, *Titanic*, p. 36.

77. Quoted in Marcus, *The Maiden Voyage*, p. 169.

78. Quoted in Gracie, *Titanic*, p. 107.

79. Quoted in Walter Lord, *A Night to Remember*. New York: Bantam, 1955, p. 117.

80. Lord, *A Night to Remember*, p. 117.

81. Quoted in Davie, *Titanic*, pp. 121–22.

82. Quoted in Lord, *A Night to Remember*, p. 118.

83. Quoted in Marcus, *The Maiden Voyage*, pp. 196–97.

Chapter 7: How Could This Happen?

84. Quoted in Lord, *The Night Lives On*, p. 28.

85. Quoted in Lord, *A Night to Remember*, p. 130.

86. Quoted in Lord, *The Night Lives On*, p. 13.

87. Quoted in Cowles, *The Astors*, p. 144.

88. Quoted in Eaton and Haas, *Titanic*, p. 98.

89. Quoted in Eaton and Haas, *Titanic*, p. 99.

90. Quoted in *Titanic, the Official Story, April 14–15, 1912*. p. 2.

91. Quoted in Jessop with Maxtone-Graham, *Titanic Survivor*, p. 12.

92. Quoted in Marcus, *The Maiden Voyage*, p. 205.

93. Quoted in Lord, *The Night Lives On*, p. 198.

94. Lynch, *Titanic*, p. 118.

95. Quoted in Lord, *The Night Lives On*, pp. 71–72.

96. Quoted in Davie, *Titanic*, p. 32.

Chapter 8: Unending Fascination

97. Quoted in J. D. Reed and Simon Perry, "Spared by the Sea," *People*, May 19, 1997, p. 112.

98. Quoted in Reed and Perry, "Spared by the Sea," p. 112.

99. Jessop with Maxtone-Graham, *Titanic Survivor*, p. 11.

100. Lord, *The Night Lives On*, p. 16.

101. Lord, *The Night Lives On*, p. 16.

102. Lord, *The Night Lives On*, p. 238.

103. Ballard, *Exploring the Titanic*, p. 30.

104. Quoted in Davie, *Titanic*, p. 215.

105. Quoted in Lord, *The Night Lives On*, p. 239.

106. Robert D. Ballard, "Epilogue for the *Titanic*," *National Geographic*, October 1987, p. 462.

107. Quoted in Ballard, *Exploring the Titanic*, p. 60.

108. Quoted in Lynch, *Titanic*, p. 208.

109. Quoted in Richard O'Connor, *The Golden Summers*. New York: G. P. Putnam's Sons, 1974, pp. 208–209.

110. Quoted in Davie, *Titanic*, p. 59.

Facts About the Titanic

At 46,328 gross tons, the *Titanic* was 50 percent larger than any other working ship of its day.

She measured 883 feet long from front to back.

At her widest part (the middle), the *Titanic* was 92.5 feet across.

She carried 3,500 bags of mail and 900 tons of baggage.

Her height of 104 feet was comparable to an 11-story building.

Her smokestacks measured, on average, 62 feet high and 22 feet across.

Three million rivets were used to hold the ship together.

The boilers on the ship were more than 15 feet high.

There were 3 propellers on the ship: 2 measured over 23 feet while the center propeller was 16 feet across.

Her rudder weighed 101 tons.

The ship had 29 boilers and 159 furnaces for power.

She was the first ship to be fitted with a Parsons turbine, giving increased power without requiring more steam.

The ship sunk about 400 miles off the coast of Newfoundland.

The ice field that downed the *Titanic* was 78 miles long.

For Further Reading

Books

Robert D. Ballard, *Exploring the Titanic.* New York: Madison, 1989. Absorbing firsthand account of the 1985 and 1986 expeditions that succeeded in locating, then exploring, the remains of the *Titanic.* Numerous illustrations, including black-and-white contemporary photos, paintings, and color photos of the expedition and wreckage site, which the author explored on the ocean floor.

Tom Kuntz, ed., *The Titanic Disaster Hearings: The Official Transcripts of the 1912 Senate Investigation.* New York: Pocket Books, 1998. Nearly six hundred pages of firsthand accounts by people who testified before Senator William A. Smith's investigative committee shortly after the disaster. Witnesses include passengers, crew members, and experts on shipbuilding, navigation, and telegraphy; the captains and crews from other ships, including the *Carpathia* and the *Californian*; and others.

Walter Lord, *A Night to Remember.* New York: Bantam, 1955. A popular dramatic account of April 12 and the immediate aftermath of the *Titanic* disaster, with many quotes and anecdotes.

Walter Lord, *The Night Lives On.* New York: William Morrow, 1986. An absorbing look at some lingering questions and issues surrounding the *Titanic* disaster; updates on the author's earlier research.

Don Lynch, *Titanic: An Illustrated History.* Toronto: Madison, 1992. Richly illustrated, detailed account of the life and times of the *Titanic*—its creation, passengers and crew, voyage, sinking, rescue, and aftermath. Later chapters cover lingering questions, the discovery and exploration of its remains in the 1980s, and the "*Titanic* legacy." A colorful foldout center section allows readers to "tour the ship."

Robert A. Rosenbaum, ed., *Best Book of True Ship Stories.* New York: Doubleday, 1966. Fascinating maritime adventures based on firsthand accounts, including one by the second mate on the *Carpathia* when it rescued the *Titanic* survivors.

Frank Sloan, *Titanic.* New York: Franklin Watts, 1987. For young people. Clear, interesting coverage of the voyage and sinking of the *Titanic* and the rescue; includes some material on the discovery and exploration of the wreckage in 1985 and 1986.

———, *Titanic: The Official Story, April 14–15, 1912.* New York: Random House, 1997. A boxed collection of reproductions of documents related to the *Titanic* from the London Public Record Office; government certificates, letters, contemporary newspaper accounts, the original deck plans, the final telegram for help, and more.

Articles

Robert D. Ballard, "Epilogue for the *Titanic*," *National Geographic*, October 1987, pp. 454–63. Pictorial feature showing the wreckage explored in 1986; explanatory text by Ballard, director of the Woods Hole Oceanographic Institution and leader of the group that entered the wreckage site in the manned submersible *Alvin*.

Robert D. Ballard, "How We Found *Titanic*," *National Geographic*, December 1985, pp. 696–719. An account of the finding of the *Titanic*.

Works Consulted

Robert D. Ballard, *The Discovery of the Titanic*. New York: Warner, 1987. Fascinating step-by-step description of the author's successful attempts to find and explore the site of the famous ship, a goal he accomplished in 1985 and 1986; wonderful color photos, paintings, and diagrams.

Lawrence Beesley, *The Loss of the S.S. Titanic: Its Story and Its Lessons*. Boston: Houghton Mifflin, 1912. Evenhanded, straightforward account by a teacher who was a Second Class passenger on the *Titanic* and survived in one of its lifeboats.

Shan F. Bullock, *A Titanic Hero: Thomas Andrews, Shipbuilder*. Riverside, CT: 7 C's Press, 1912. Reprint 1973. The life and death of the talented, courageous chief ship designer at Harland & Wolff who went down with the *Titanic*, which he helped to create.

Virginia Cowles, *The Astors*. New York: Knopf, 1979. Colorful history of this wealthy, influential American family—their commercial enterprises, lifestyles, family life, and impact on high society, especially in New York City and Newport, Rhode Island.

Michael Davie, *Titanic: The Death and Life of a Legend*. New York: Knopf, 1987. A thorough account of the *Titanic* disaster; beginning with historical material about the shipbuilding and steamship industries; then discussing the aftermath, inquests, lawsuits, lives of survivors, and discovery of the wreckage in the mid-1980s.

John P. Eaton and Charles A. Haas, *Titanic: Destination Disaster, the Legends and the Reality*. New York: Norton, 1987. Numerous black-and-white photos relating to the disaster and the discovery of the wreckage.

Archibald Gracie, *Titanic: A Survivor's Story*. Chicago: Academy, 1913. Reprint 1986. An engrossing contemporary account by a gallant man who helped passengers board lifeboats, then managed to swim to safety after going down with the ship; unique material obtained from interviewing survivors.

William Hoffman and Jack Grimm, *Beyond Reach: The Search for the Titanic*. New York: Beaufort, 1982. Grimm, an oil tycoon, geologist, and financier, describes his three attempts to locate the wreckage of the *Titanic*, interspersed with stories about the ship's history and its tragic maiden voyage.

Violet Jessop with John Maxtone-Graham, ed., *Titanic Survivor*. Dobbs Ferry, NY: Sheridan House, 1997. A fascinating look at steamship travel and the night of April 14–15 from the viewpoint of a career stewardess who went on to survive the *Britannic* disaster as well.

Charles H. Lightoller, *Titanic and Other Ships*. London: Nicholson and Watson,

1935. A memoir of the *Titanic*'s second officer, who survived on an overturned collapsible lifeboat after going down with his ship. It includes a seaman's outlook on steamship travel and methods of navigation before and after the *Titanic* disaster.

Geoffrey Marcus, *The Maiden Voyage*. New York: Viking, 1969. An extensive account of the *Titanic*'s only voyage, beginning with the morning of April 12, 1912. Contains many quotations and analyses and coverage of both the U.S. and British inquests.

Anthony Masters, ed. *Heroic Stories*. New York: Kingfisher, 1994. A collection of readings that describe heroic actions by people in dangerous or personally challenging situations. Included is an excerpt from Colonel Archibald Gracie's book about his experiences during the *Titanic* disaster.

Byron S. Miller, *Sail, Steam, and Splendour*. New York: Times Books, 1977. A fascinating look at the history of shipbuilding and the shipping industry.

Richard O'Connor, *The Golden Summers*. New York: G. P. Putnam's Sons, 1974. A look at the lifestyles and private lives of the wealthy and socially prominent people who made up Newport society during the years between 1890 and 1914.

Peter Padfield, *The Titanic and the Californian*. New York: John Day, 1965. An intensive look at the ongoing controversy about the location and behavior of the Leyland liner the *Californian*. The author brings out facts and little-known evidence that would show that Captain Lord was not guilty of misconduct on that fateful night.

J. D. Reed and Simon Perry, "Spared by the Sea," *People*, May 19, 1997, p. 112. An interview with Millvina Dean, who survived the sinking of the *Titanic* along with her mother and brother when she was an infant.

Joseph J. Thorndike Jr., *The Very Rich: A History of Wealth*. New York: American Heritage, 1976. Heavily illustrated book about wealthy people, the origins of their wealth, and their lifestyles; includes material about the Astors and other wealthy First Class passengers on the *Titanic*.

Jack Winocour, ed., *The Story of the Titanic as Told by Its Survivors*. New York: Dover, 1960. Includes interviews with four survivors, including wireless operator Harold Bride.

Index

Picture Credits

Cover photo: Popperfoto/Archive Photos

AP/Wide World Photos, 88, 95, 96

Archive Photos, 23, 24, 27, 35, 39, 40, 43, 45, 58, 60, 68, 77, 89

From Braynard, *Story of the "Titanic" Post-cards,* a Dover Publication, 10, 20, 21, 81, 84

Corbis-Bettmann, 52, 57, 75

European Photo/FPG International, 48

Library of Congress, 16

Bert & Richard Morgan/Archive Photos, 87

New York Times/Archive Photos, 78

Pach/Corbis-Bettmann, 15

Popperfoto/Archive Photos, 12, 42, 55

Underwood & Underwood/Corbis-Bettmann, 30, 36, 37, 51

UPI/Corbis-Bettmann, 25, 28, 31, 33, 34, 54, 61, 64, 66, 67, 69, 71, 73, 94

About the Author

Victoria Sherrow holds B.S. and M.S. degrees from Ohio State University. Among her writing credits are numerous stories and articles, twelve books of fiction, and more than forty works of nonfiction for children and young adults. Her recent books have explored such topics as biomedical ethics, the Great Depression, the Holocaust, and the Gold Rush.

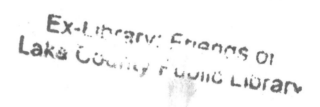

Ex-Library: Friends of
Lake County Public Library

910.91634 SHER   HO
Sherrow, Victoria.
The Titanic

LAKE COUNTY PUBLIC LIBRARY
INDIANA

AD	FF	MU
AV	GR	NC
BO	HI	SJ
CL	HO MAY 19 '99	CN L
DS	LS	

THIS BOOK IS RENEWABLE BY PHONE OR IN PERSON IF THERE IS NO RESERVE
WAITING OR FINE DUE.   LCP #0390